W9-CHF-548

ROMANTIC INNS
OF
M E X I C O

ROMANTIC INNS
OF
MEXICO

A SELECTIVE GUIDE TO
CHARMING ACCOMMODATIONS
SOUTH OF THE BORDER

TOBY SMITH

CHRONICLE BOOKS • SAN FRANCISCO

Copyright © 1986 by Toby Smith.
All rights reserved. No part of this book
may be reproduced in any form without
written permission from the publisher.
Printed in the United States of America.

Library of Congress Cataloging in
Publication Data
Smith, Toby, 1946–
    Romantic inns of Mexico

    1. Hotels, taverns, etc.—Mexico—
Directories.
I. Title.
TX910.M6S6   1986   647'.947201
85-17153
ISBN 0-87701-333-0

Editing: Rain Blockley
Book & cover design: Fearn Cutler
Typography: On Line Typography
Cover Photo: Courtesy Barbara &
Richard Henderson, owners of Quinta
Quetzalcóatl, Lake Chapala, Mexico
Photography: Ray Smith
10 9 8 7 6 5 4 3 2 1

Chronicle Books
One Hallidie Plaza
San Francisco, CA 94102

Contents

Acknowledgments

I would like to credit Barbi Henderson, co-owner of The Plumed Serpent, or Quinta Quetzalcóatl, for apprising me of many of the inns described in this book. Her travel tours through central Mexico unearthed enough leads to form a nucleus for my research. California innkeepers who helpfully supplied information on specific inns are Ann Swett of the Old Monterey Inn and Tom Haworth, Vintage Towers. My thanks also to Marion McMurtry, Fran Carroll, and Susan Schwartz—frequent travelers in Mexico.

This book would have been impossible without the patient help of Ray Smith, my photographer, fact verifier, and husband. Fran Bigelow kindly checked with me Spanish spellings, phrases, and their English equivalents. And it would have been insubmissible without the fine-tuning of my friend, journalism instructor Geets Vincent.

Preface

I t might occur to you while gazing, open mouthed, at the ruins of a 2,000-year-old acropolis of a vanished race at Oaxaca's Monte Albán. Or off the coast of the Yucatán, snorkeling through clear, aqua waters among a school of vibrantly colored parrot fish. Perhaps an appreciation of the many facets of historic and ruggedly beautiful Mexico might begin as an inkling while you traverse the stark, boulder-strewn length of the Baja California highway. Or as you fly in at night, over the rim of mountains that hold Mexico City and its some 13 million souls.

Mexico's ancient history has largely been bypassed this century. Instead, we learn about China as it was 3,000 years ago, Egypt and its antiquities, and the roots of other emerging Third World countries. Yet Mexico is in the same league. Mayan ruins date from the days of the sphinx, and the culture that created them was as sophisticated if not more so.

One reason for visiting this historic country to our south is the people. From San Miguel de Allende, where residents are used to *gringos* with no second language, to Pátzcuaro, trade center for neighboring Indian villages and only an occasional wandering North American, all were cordial. Once I brought out a small English–Spanish phrase book and tried a tenuous sentence, there were no bounds to the enthusiasm with which my Mexican counterpart would try to figure out what I wanted to communicate.

And then there are the bargains. I could have refurnished my home—or even stocked an import shop—with the excellent quality hand-crafted originals we saw on three research trips below the border. Large, serenely colored woolen rugs woven in a village near Pátzcuaro for around $15; hand-designed silver jewelry from Taxco at around $30 an ounce; more sophisticated pottery pieces at San Miguel de Allende; distinctive yarn dolls of costumed Indian dancers near Oaxaca for a few dollars— these are good buys despite the peso's shifting value. Although devaluation, inflation and government controls cloud the exact rates for goods, food, and rooms, be assured of one thing: They are generally incredibly lower than in the United States.

The pleasure of returning again and again to various parts of Mexico is heightened by the discovery of historic and/ or romantic inns, hidden away behind nondescript walls and down back roads. These are establishments whose separate parts come together like ingredients of a perfect *margarita* on a hot day after a dusty drive. No longer is it necessary to stay in those high-rise chains and eat in poor copies of U.S. coffee shops and hotel restaurants.

It is often difficult to learn of these establishments. Travel agents are frequently turned off by larger hotels that overbook, which leaves the agents with angry clients. Smaller places seldom pay commissions to agents, another roadblock. In most automobile club listings and travel books, a few inns are lumped in helter-skelter with high-rises and motels. And finally, smaller places have a word-of-mouth following but no funds for advertising.

There are inns in Mexico. Many are run by English-speaking Americans or Europeans who realize bath towels, if not washcloths, are necessities in bathrooms; that making a reservation in advance for a certain room means that room should be available when guests arrive; and that *gringos* just can't hack the local water. Even so, there is quite a difference between North American and Mexican inns.

A more descriptive word for the latter is *quinta*, meaning "fifth." In the 1800s, Mexican settlements were scattered hundreds of miles from each other across desolate mountain ranges. Travelers would ride hard for four days, then rest at an inn on the fifth. Those inns became known as *quintas*, according to Mike Eager, one of the new breed of innkeeper in Mexico, and the term covers the variety of accommodations now available. The inns we have discovered to date vary from relatively new ones, as elegant as many in this country and with a handful of rooms, to ancient *haciendas* with more than a hundred rooms on historic grounds. The establishments described here are in interesting locations, where the novice traveler with little or no Spanish will feel comfortable.

Room rates are indicated at the end of each entry. For the purposes of this book, expensive inns are those that charge $100 or more per day, double occupancy; moderate, $40 to $99; and inexpensive, under $39. Keep in mind that actual rates range from more than $200 to less than $15, and that some include meals.

Despite criss-crossing Mexico three times, we were unable to include every romantic inn. Some were too far off our route, some opened after our last trip, and some we just couldn't find because of language or time constraints. For these reasons, I would love to hear from readers about other accommodations that may be suitable for inclusion in future editions.

Even though the inns described in these pages are safe, comfortable oases from which to explore the country's culture, this is not to say you'll never encounter a goof on a reservation, the trots, or a cockroach. I for one would avoid bringing a pregnant woman to Mexico for basic reasons: occasional noxious odors such as auto lubricating oil; frequently nonfunctioning public rest rooms; and the inability to communicate specific food choices. On the other hand, any adventurous soul willing to leave the time-management calendar home and convert to a more leisurely attitude toward events of the day will have a wonderful time. A stay in Mexico develops patience and understanding of others.

I'd like to pass along a few general recommendations and a potpourri of helpful hints to the traveler.

• Pick one town or area for your visit and allow time to become thoroughly familiar with it. If you hop from inn to inn, as we did, bags may lag behind, driving to a new town every day is the pits, and you have to learn where everything is all over again.

• Make reservations early, allowing at least three weeks for a letter to reach its destination and another three weeks for the confirmation to reach you. Send a partial deposit check along to seal the deal. If you want specific information on how much to send and what room is available, call the inn and then leave time for the letter of confirmation to reach you. Phone in the morning, for that is when the chief clerk, the one most apt to understand English, will be on duty. Rooms are more in demand during high season, Christmas through May, and longer notice may be required.

• Make all your reservations before leaving home. Unless your innkeeper helps you, there is no way to phone from one inn to the next without knowing Spanish, however patient you are.

● As for phoning back to the United States, I have accomplished this only in Baja California and from the Mexico City airport, where special phones are available for long-distance calls. You insert a twenty-*centavo* piece, dial 09, and get connected with a bilingual operator.

Now for the pocketful of hints.

● Smile a lot. Carry a Spanish phrase book, pad, and pencil. Realize that if something breaks down, you can't just go down the street and get a new one. Time in Mexico is not like time in the United States.

● There is only one hour's difference between the Yucatán and Baja Sur, and another hour's difference between Baja Sur and Baja Norte.

● Read the book *Aztec* by Gary Jennings (Avon Books, 1982), a fictionalized version of Mexico's history. (I skipped the gory parts.)

● Say *por favor* ("please") a lot, and memorize the phrase *Lo siento, no entiendo*, which means, "I'm sorry, I didn't understand."

● Take with you a washcloth, a container of wipes for hands and face, and a plastic bag with handles, for wet bathing suits. Also, take enough toothpaste, laxatives, and kaopectate so you won't have to waste a day of vacation trying to find a drugstore where English is spoken. Products are often labeled differently as well.

● Don't drive out of town after dark. Cows sleep on the road, and other animals and people are hard to see. If you have an accident, you may be thrown in jail for months—and there are few witnesses to what happens after dark. In certain sections of Mexico, you might also encounter certain undesirable characters who don't like anyone, let alone Americans.

During the day, roads are much safer. And Mexico's Ministry of Tourism provides a fleet of green pickup trucks to assist drivers who have car trouble on the main roads between 8 A.M. and 9 P.M. The service is free; parts are sold at cost. The fleet's English-speaking drivers are well versed in first aid, sightseeing attractions, and tourist facilities in their respective areas.

- You can safely buy food at markets as long as it has a disposable skin, such as oranges and bananas. The same goes for beverages, meaning (wiped dry) cans or bottles.

- Ask the inn manager about local haggling practices and taxi fares before venturing out.

- If you're not sure about a restaurant, order soup and bread and dine like a king.

- Change your money to *pesos* at the government-run Bank of Mexico in the airports to save time and to get the best rate.

- If you plan to buy things for your home, measure floors, walls, etc. before your trip.

- Mexican beer is excellent, with less carbonation and more flavor than our own. *Margaritas* run the gamut. (After visiting this sometimes sweltering country, the reader may better understand the frequent mention of this cooling concoction.)

- Don't walk barefoot to the bathroom in the middle of the night, even in the poshest inn. That's when the wily granddaddy cockroaches take a walk.

And then relax, keep your eyes and ears open, and enjoy the experience.

ROMANTIC INNS
OF
M E X I C O

I

Yucatán

Just where does one start a book on romantic Mexican inns? In the high central region, the Colonial Circle, where the weather is always great and the architecture astounding? The newer west coast, the so-called Mexican Riviera? Baja, the last area to be settled and developed?

After much thought, perhaps ten minutes, the Yucatán won out. It's a personal decision. I love everything about this isolated eastern peninsula: its part in Mexico's ancient history, its preservation of its own distinctive character, its first-class snorkeling, and its friendly people. Perhaps isolation has contributed to its flavor. A big toe of land sticking up into the Gulf of Mexico, it is nearly cut off from the rest of Mexico by Guatemala.

Spaniards—who were to play such a long, dominant role in this country—first landed on Yucatán's eastern shores. Imagine their wonder at stumbling across great cities of stone structures, many already deserted and crowded in by jungle. Reasons for the mass exodus, first of Maya Indians and then their conquerers, the Toltecs, are still unknown.

Azure water laps at beaches and white sand as fine as any in the Caribbean islands can be found here, along with spots that offer unparalleled snorkeling and jungle so thick often you can't see twenty feet beyond the road. Unsolved mysteries as old as the Egyptian sphinx continue to baffle amateurs as well as trained archeologists who study Mayan and Toltec ruins.

It is easy to get around in the Yucatán. Mérida, its capital, and Cancún, destination of most foreigners, each have jet airports and are only about two hundred miles apart. Roads are straight, for the countryside is hilly at most. You can rent cars at either of the two major population centers or take one of many buses. Some visitors hitchhike, an acceptable practice here.

The Yucatán climate is tropical, especially during the rainy season, July through September, making air conditioning or good ventilation an important consideration for a good night's sleep.

More than anything, it is the people of the Yucatán that make it a special place for me. With soft, black wavy hair above almond shaped eyes in round faces frequently creased with smiles, many are descendents of ancient Mayans who built great cities in the Yucatán a thousand years ago. Joyous, sharing, and proud of their Mayan roots, parents keep their culture alive by teaching youngsters the old tales and dances. Even though many still live in one-room thatched huts with dirt floors, men, women, and children wear the spotless white cotton shirts and pants and embroidered dresses peculiar to this region—and popular purchases among visitors.

There is a sense of humor in casual contact, missing in many harsher parts of the country. It is a pleasure to converse with these people. On a bus headed toward Cancún, for example, we talked with a group of high school boys. Considering the language barrier, it was more like writing notes. With the aid of an English–Spanish phrase book, our constant companion, we were able to find out the names and ages of all five boys, their favorite baseball teams, players, types of car, and other vital statistics. In the United States, teenagers do not often converse in a foreign language with strangers decades older than themselves. But these boys handled the situation as naturally as if it happened every week. They were on vacation from school and their destination was Cancún, the same as that of many of their U.S. counterparts.

Cancún is a tourist-oriented coastal town near the tip of the Yucatán peninsula. But if you dig deeper you will find Akumal, Cobá, and Chichén Itzá, natural wonders for your enjoyment.

Club Akumal Caribe

This book may at times seem top-heavy with fantastic romantic hotels, perfectly appointed rooms, and impeccable cuisine. Club Akumal Caribe, near Cancún in the Yucatán, is here for a different, though just as romantic and fantastic, reason. Let's start by sitting at the bar, situated on the white, hand-swept sand of a half-mile, crescent shaped beach. The friendly bartender speaks slowly, so you can understand his Spanish greeting, "*¿Cómo está usted?*" ("how are you?") then switches to good English to make it easier for you. The music is standard Top Forty from home, in English. Sand trickles between your toes as you sit on rough stools and order something big and refreshing. The large circular bar is shaded by a conical thatched roof supported every four feet by earthen loaf-shaped berms. Two double *margaritas* thunk down on a well-weathered wooden plank bar. Icy cold, not the greatest, but reasonable.

A sailboat and three skiffs bob at anchor in the blue, blue Caribbean waters. You calculate that, by hopping from the shade of one coconut palm to the next, you can walk the length of the beach without scorching the bottoms of your feet. Palms of every age are growing all over. Flattened by a late summer hurricane, a few live on as natural benches.

People with bathing suits, fins, and face masks descend stone steps at the bay's northernmost end to snorkel. They yell to each other about fish seen below, and you promise to follow their example later. Gentle waves lap at the raked water line. A light sea breeze clears the air, keeping tropical insects further inland. Altogether, only a few dozen people are in evidence at the bar and along the beach.

This is it. This is the tropical paradise you've dreamed about. Why is everybody else crammed onto that long spit of land an hour's drive north, Cancún, waiting in lines, taking elevators to room 909?

Here you have two restaurants from which to choose. Next to the bar is a thatched-roof restaurant and bar built close to the sand. Palms grow up through the room and the roof. Under the screened windows are sunken cages filled with pheasants and peacocks roosting on branches as night gathers. The rest of the decor is simple—red and white checkered cloths on tables—and entrées are limited. But how many choices do you need when two of them are lobster? Add a bowl of soup and the tab comes to about $15 each.

The main dining room, which seats fifty or more, is a circle of white stucco arches topped with a huge thatched dome, located on a small rise at the end of the beach. Doors are left open to the ocean. Tapes of international favorites play, in Spanish. Prices are reasonable. As you walk back along the beach at night, a few fireflies and, more dependable, small tiki lights guide your way.

The snorkeling turns out to be so-so, but a few miles farther south is a national underwater park with schools of parrot fish and other beauties (see Cobá, the next entry). Eleventh-century ruins at Tulúm, one of the last cities built by the Mayans, are small enough to comprehend but spectacular enough to impress. They are just south of the park.

Akumal offers three choices of lodging: hotel room, beachfront condominium, and hut. The latter two complexes adjoin each other. The hotel is out of sight, farther down the beach.

We chose a hut, after reading in a Mexico travel book that they were quaint Mayan huts. That's a misnomer. These are square, natural rock cabins, two per unit, with a single large room, about sixteen feet square; and full bath, which is tiled and has an open shower. The double bed is on a pedestal, as is the colorfully pillowed sofa. Built-in end tables with nonfunctioning lights, a round wooden table, and armchairs complete the furnishings. Along one wall are shelves, a closet, and a mini-kitchen: hot plates, sink, small refrigerator, and a big bottle of purified water on a stand. Tile floors and white walls are clean, and an overhead fan keeps you cool.

Three sides have large screened openings, covered with green slatted blinds that crank open. You'll want them open most of the time, trading off the visual protection from passersby for the ocean breezes and the lulling sound of little waves hitting the beach.

Not your typical deluxe accommodations. But definitely romantic, and reasonable.

Akumal (meaning "place of the turtles"—although the turtles no longer come) was discovered about ten years ago by some Texans who built the improvements as well as a skin diving center near the larger restaurant. Somehow the property became divided, with one manager for the condos, or *casitas*, and another for the forty more primitive huts. If you want a hut, talk to the manager in the office to the right of the white entry gate; the man in the left office handles the *casitas*. The condos are strung out in a one-story line; each has two bedrooms, two baths, a sitting room, kitchenette area, and private patio.

It seems to smack of a big land development scheme that didn't jell. How fortunate for us romantics with limited resources.

For huts: Club Akumal Caribe "Villas Maya," Apartado Postal 984, Cancún, Quintana Roo, Mexico. Telephone (800) 351-1622. Anni Kunzi, bilingual manager. 40 units in huts. Inexpensive. Overhead fans. Note—for the condominiums available at Akumal write: Las Casitas de Akumal, P.O. Box 714, Cancún, Quintana Roo, Mexico. Telephone (operator assisted) 4-19-45 or 4-16-89. Don Mincey, resident manager.

Villa Arqueologica

I will never forget one fall afternoon in 1978. We'd spent most of a week's vacation on the coast of the Yucatán Peninsula with another couple and decided to loop south to see the spectacular ruins at Tulúm. This smaller site is less overpowering than others, yet impressive. Not only are the ruins photogenic, but a beautiful white sandy beach stretches below and provides occasional sightings of nude bathers.

Out on a high point with uninterrupted vision in three directions and a wall on the fourth, Tulúm was a fortified Mayan city, one of the last of many constructed in the Yucatán. Unlike more ancient sites with buildings grouped around plazas, Tulúm resembles a small modern city, with buildings along straight streets. Perhaps it was built at a time when the Mayans felt more threatened. But we may never know, for very little decipherable history is available to experts about the Mayan civilization and its demise.

From Tulúm, we drove inland about thirty miles to a wide loop in the road with a few thatched huts here and there. That was—and is—Cobá. We couldn't find the ruins noted in our guidebook, nor any way out except the way we came. But at the end of one of the few side streets, by the edge of a nice lake, we found a rambling two-story, bright white stucco hotel. It was immaculate—and empty. Linens and wine glasses graced the dining room, the pool was filled, flowery shrubs grew in the central patio, staff was at the ready. But no guests. I was sure we'd stumbled across the secret hideaway of the Mexican Mafia, if there is such a thing.

That was seven years ago. I could hardly wait to return when researching for this book. But what a letdown. What we thought was a secret meeting place is actually one of five Villas

Arqueologicas built by Club Med near the most visited ruins in the Yucatán and Mexico City. These establishments are sedate, comfortable cocoons in which to retire after a day of climbing crumbling temple steps here or at Tulúm in the tropical heat. And I mean retire. Unlike other Club Med destination resorts, which require memberships and provide rounds of activities and facilities for children, the Villa Arqueologica closes everything, even the bar, by 10:15 P.M.

The two Club Meds where I stayed, here and at Chichén Itzá, are practically interchangeable. A shallow L-shaped pool and thatch-covered patio occupy the lush courtyard, which is paved with unglazed tiles. On three sides of the courtyard, a covered walkway leads to the rooms. On the fourth are the dining room, bar, gift shop, and entry. Above the white stuccoed columns stands another floor of rooms, all topped by the Spanish tiled roof.

Rooms are a series of white plaster niches and arches with built-in furniture. Each single bed is in a separate well-lit niche. An innerspring mattress rests on a built-in platform, covered with a warmly colored woven spread. Above a window seat, matching drapes hang at the picture window, which overlooks the jungle outside. A modern bathroom contains Eurobath liquid soap in the shower. Walls are thick and ceilings low, so

Villa Arqueologica Cobá, S.P. 710, Cancún, Quintana Roo, Mexico. Raul Robles Rivera, manager. *Reservations:* **Agencia Operadora Club Med, Calle Leibnitz 34, Mexico, D.F. 11590. Telephone (operator assisted) 533-4800; telex 01771032** CMEDME. **40 rooms. Inexpensive. Air-conditioned.**

the air conditioner works well. And all the jungle bugs are safely outside.

The air-conditioned dining room is similarly sealed off from the jungle. Menu listings make the mouth water, but the few entries we tried could have used a little more imagination in the kitchen. Reproductions from the famous Museum of Archeology in Mexico City are in the comfortable, large dining room and in hall niches. Many are for sale in the small gift shop, as are sundries.

Decorations in the bar run to blow-ups of old Zapata photos and civil war guns, the same as in the Chichén Itzá bar.

The ruins, which we found this time, are unrestored, spread out, and unimpressive compared to the more accessible ones at Tulúm, Chichén Itzá, and elsewhere. However, archeologists feel Cobá was a more important, central city in the network of settlements. The entrance to the jungle trails between ruins is about a block from the Club Med, beyond a dirt parking lot and small sign. We walked quite a way, encountering only one large stone base, like the bottom steps of a pyramid, with mature trees growing from the treads. But it might be fun to rent bikes at the hut near the park entrance and ride the trails between sites.

These Club Med hotels provide a service for the country by supplying reasonably priced accommodations for international travelers; they can depend on cleanliness and good service. Guests come by the busloads. We saw a French group fill a practically empty dining room and then ran across another large group on a daytime tour.

If you do travel to this backroads spot—the road now goes through to the inland—be sure to visit Tulúm and Xel-ha (pronounced shell-ha). Just a few miles north of Tulúm, Xel-ha is an archeological park with an underwater museum where you snorkel among fancifully colored tropical fish—the best snorkeling I've seen in Mexico. The park is set around a deep slit in the shoreline, lined with volcanic rock for fish to use for cover and to hunt food. Seawater fills the inlet and surrounds the little islands of rock, but the area is protected from heavy surf. Perhaps the slit was another Mayan innovation.

You can see many fish from the shores of this long arm of water, but best of all is to slip right into the water with them. There are changing rooms and snorkels for rent right there, or you may bring your own equipment. Paddle through the split in a small rocky outcropping in the bay. I've never seen a whole school of parrot fish before, or since, my visit there.

Hotel Hacienda Chichén

M y initial contact with Indian ruins in Mexico was in the Yucatán, at Chichén Itzá (chee-CHEN ee-TSAH). Everyone who ever clambers up and down one of those ancient sites has his or her own unforgettable experience of the impact of history. I spent my first morning of awe eight years ago, long before starting to write about inns. By noon that day, absolutely overwhelmed, we came by accident to Hacienda Chichén. In the very shadow of the ruins, surrounded by jungle, stands what was once the stately home of Edward Thompson, U.S. Ambassador to Mexico before the turn of the century and until 1924. He bought the historic site for less than $100 in 1885 and spent years poking around, especially down in the sacrificial pool or water-filled cavern where bodies and possessions were thrown.

The site was given back to the Mexican Department of Antiquities which has since restored the newer buildings to the north. The high-ceilinged mansion, actually built in the 1600s, is now the dining room, kitchen, office, and sitting room of this fine hostlery. The sprawling white stucco building is entered via wide stairs and a series of arches balanced on delicate columns. On a screened patio beyond the formal entry, we lunched on a clear chicken soup and excellent Mexican rolls—a delicious and safe order nearly anywhere in the country, although there were many other offerings here. An exceptionally attentive and patient staff waited as we tried to decipher the menu.

A dozen boxy, rustic cabins, once used for Thompson's many friends and visiting dignitaries, are in front of the building. Suites are named for some of these visitors, who no doubt returned home with some priceless and irreplaceable Mayan and Toltec artifacts. The two single-story units in each cabin face in opposite directions, so the paved, open veranda of each is private. From some you can catch glimpses of the tops of ruins, above the verdant jungle. Others are near the large tiled swimming pool. Each suite has a full tiled bath and will eventually contain new cooling fans, wiring, paint, and furnishings.

On my most recent visit, Hacienda Chichén was closed for extensive sprucing up. I talked to the manager, Oscar Manzur, who said the cabins would remain the same structurally but be much improved. He assured me the job would be completed by winter 1985; you might call to check before your trip.

Clustered along paths around the *hacienda's* gardens are the

Hotel Hacienda Chichén, Chichén Itzá, Yucatán, Mexico. Oscar Manzur, manager. *Reservations:* Mérida Travel Service, P.O. Box 407, Calle 55, No. 510, Mérida, Yucatán, Mexico. Telephone (operator assisted) 1-92-12; telex 753841. 20 Units. Inexpensive. Fans only.

older Mayan buildings. They are crumbling more than those a few yards to the north, and their promenades are less distinguishable. Launched around 450 A.D., the city included church buildings and an amazing several-storied cylindrical building that was an observatory. Restored structures across what once was the road show how later Toltec tribes built pyramids right over the Mayan ones. You can see the different architectural features, especially notable around stone doorways. You may enter one pyramid through a narrow passageway; at its inner core is a life-sized carved stone jaguar with green stones for eyes. This particular pyramid also has a total of 365 steps, the same number as the days in our modern calendars. Most remarkable, on certain days of the year, shadows on the steps of one side of the building reportedly form the shape of a descending dragon!

Another remarkable sight is a flat area as large as a football field whose stone walls are painted with scenes of warriors being killed. A small vertical stone hoop high on one wall was used by teams who tossed a small ball through it. And at one end of this expanse, from a small covered platform, a person speaking in a normal tone of voice can be heard the length of the field.

Staying at Hacienda Chichén, you can explore one building at a time and come out with a better understanding of it all.

Hotel Mayaland

Another romantic place to stay within sight of the Chichén Itzá ruins is this 1930s hotel with a 1970 addition. Built in the grand style of the time, with marble and arches, the plant-filled lobby with fountain soars up two stories. A wide marble staircase to the second-floor balcony is rimmed with graceful wrought iron railings. Conversational groupings of chairs and end tables are set about on the balcony.

Rooms of the older section are in this wing, off a covered arcade the length of the structure. All are spacious and have fancy tiled floors. Large ceiling fans and wood-shuttered and screened windows provide good ventilation. On the side toward the ruins, beyond shuttered French doors, are screened porches with chairs and tables. The room we saw had a built-in king-sized bed, long mirrored dresser, end tables, a convenient place to hang clothes, and in the tiled bathroom, a walk-in shower.

Newer units in a four-story wing are also large, containing a sofa sitting area as well as a patio. Beige tiles cover the floor, but the bath is conventional white tile with precast shower/tub. Furnishings are the same as in the historic wing, and the curtain material is like the brightly colored embroidered dresses favored by Yucatán women.

I found a third type of room, available only during cooler winter months, while wandering around Mayaland's lush tropical gardens with their spraying fountain centerpiece. A dozen authentic-looking Mayan huts lie here and there among the overgrown plants. Similar simple one-room adobe rectangles with rounded corners and dried palm-leaf roofs are home for most Yucatán families. Often hammocks are hung in the corners—the region is known for its excellent hemp, and many lightweight string hammocks go home in tourists' bags. Floors of native huts are often hard, swept dirt.

The Mayaland garden huts are tiled, and regular twin beds, end tables, and other hotel accoutrements are in place. But the roofs are thatched, with flowering vines growing in them, and the walls curve at the corners. It would be a real kick to approximate the feeling of staying in a native hut.

While the sixty-two rooms and garden area are lush and tropical in feeling, the pool area, for some reason, seemed sterile. I moved on quickly to the dining room, where high

Hotel Mayaland, Chichén Itzá, Yucatán, Mexico. *Reservations:* Mérida Travel Service, P.O. Box 407, Calle 55, No. 510, Mérida, Yucatán, Mexico. Telephone (operator assisted) 1-92-12; telex 753841. 62 rooms and suites. Inexpensive. Fans only.

ceilings, heavy timbers, and stained glass windows on two sides bring you close to the environment of Chichén Itzá. A vivid mural depicting Mayan history covers a third wall.

Some entrées offered here include venison. Yucatán is known not only for lobster and other seafood, but for deer meat. The animals have plenty to eat in the jungle, and you often see one or two men riding bicycles down the side of a main road, carrying rifles. I kept wondering how they would load their prey onto the old bikes but never spotted a successful hunter and therefore am still in the dark.

In the hotel's bar, carved panels display a panorama of all the ruins of Chichén Itzá, including some ruins not in the park proper. The work is artistic and seems in proper proportion. It would be most helpful to persons staying a week or so, who want to see everything.

On returning to the lobby from the rear of the building, one learns why Mayaland was placed as it was on this uneven terrain. Framed perfectly in the distance through the arched entry of the hotel lobby is the top of the so-called observatory, in my mind the most fantastic ruin in the whole area. This massive stone building has small slits in the wall along the circular stairway. These are designed to line up with certain stars and constellations at precise times of the year. The Mayans, whose measurement of time was very sophisticated, based their calendar and their planting season on the stars and sun. And those buildings were constructed at about the same time as the Egyptian pyramids! The architect of the Mayaland made his own subtle point in providing departing guests with this view.

Villa Arqueologica

A s noted earlier (see Villa Arqueologica, Cobá), the five villas erected by Club Med near Mexican Indian ruins are practically interchangeable. They offer sanitary, practical cubicles in which to sleep after busy days exploring ruins, and there are toothpicks in the dining room—but no washcloths in the bathrooms. They keep the bugs out of the neat compounds. They also keep out a lot of the feel of being in a foreign country. Nonetheless, they play an important part for hygiene-conscious visitors.

I always thought of Club Meds as swinging singles' vacation spas, like landlocked Love Boats. But how does one reconcile this image with the single beds, forever immovable, in white plaster niches? It is true that most Mexican hotels are furnished with twin beds, rather firm ones at that. Can it be that Mexican tradition takes precedence over full-page, full-color ad hype?

Whatever the answer, vacationing visitors do not choose Chichén Itzá for its nightlife. Everything closes up tight by 10:15, with hardly a light showing. Save that energy for Cancún or other areas of Mexico. The attraction is that whole cities of intelligent humans, in ways more advanced than their European contemporaries, inexplicably disappeared here.

Besides being comfortable and safe, the Club Med at Chichén Itzá features a large, four-foot-deep, L-shaped pool in which to relax after touring the ruins. The pool's white stucco makes the water look as true blue as ocean water over white sand. Wrought iron chaise lounges, painted white, are placed conveniently for sun devotees. Huge impatiens, hollyhocks, and other plants overflow red clay pots around the pool. Grounds are neatly kept and feature many shrubs, palms, and flowering trees.

Drinks are of good quality. A request for *cerveza* brings you an iced glass mug and a chilled local beer that even a nonbeer drinker will love.

The large restaurant's beamed ceiling presides over a pleasant Spanish atmosphere. Many replicas of Mayan artifacts are arranged on a table, as if just recovered from the ruins. The menu, in French as well as Spanish and English, includes some tony-sounding offerings. As with many chains, though, the success of their execution varies. The menu is probably dictated from a central purchasing office in Mexico City, thereby bypassing some plain and simple local specialties, such as seafood.

Meanwhile, the biggest thrill at Chichén Itzá is climbing Mayan Indian ruins and trying to imagine how life was so many centuries ago. How were the massive stepped buildings built, and why? Why did the city's people suddenly depart? Such questions have been only partially answered.

My record of climbing Mayan ruins stands at only one. It isn't terribly hard to climb the narrow treads with the long reach between steps, some a bit crumbly—it's the coming *down*. For people like me, it helps to clutch the iron handrail and descend backward.

The evening we stayed at Villa Arqueologica, a group of us returned to the ruins for a light show. It was dramatic in spite of the taped soundtrack, which wobbled and dragged, and the narration, which was in such heavily accented English as to be nearly unintelligible.

Returning through the darkened ruins, with the light of one flashlight to guide twenty people, I was thankful for the comforts of Club Med. By the time we came to the parking lot lights and passed the perfectly symmetrical tropical tree at the entrance, I was nearly running. Safe at last, I thought, as we rounded the pool.

Just then came some horrendous squawking from up in the trees. Club Med can keep the bugs out of the compound, but not the birds and/or animals. I closed the heavy door on our room with relief.

Villa Arqueologica, Chichén Itzá. *Reservations:* **Hoteles Villas Arqueologicas, Agencia Operadora Club Med, Calle Leibnitz 34, Mexico, D.F. 22590. Telephone (operator assisted) 533-4800, telex 01771032 CMEDME. 40 rooms. Inexpensive May–December, moderate December–May. Air-conditioned.**

2

Oaxaca

Visiting Oaxaca (wa-HA-cah) is like stepping through Alice in Wonderland's looking glass. This city of 127,000 people is right there on the map of central Mexico, and jets fly in and out at least once a day. But who has ever heard of it, who can pronounce it, and what are its attractions?

Alice would love it. Among the area's unbelievable sights and sounds are whistling lizards; a five-square-mile leveled mountaintop that was the Zapotec Indians' capital circa 600 A.D.; a delicately constructed retreat for rulers of the later Mixtec tribe; centuries-old open air markets, where villages are represented by their respective specialties and hard-eyed women unmercifully hustle yarn dolls at unbelievably low prices; and, at the town square several evenings a week, up to seven experienced men playing magic melodies on three *marimbas* (think of Lionel Hampton in triplicate, working the crowd) with guitar and drum backup.

Located between the Yucatán Peninsula and central Mexico but hundreds of miles from the mountain ranges that ring Mexico City, Oaxaca sits at 1,555 meters and has pleasant weather all year. You needn't worry about air-conditioning. Even during the rainy season, June through September, showers are short and strong. Just stay under cover for half an hour, then resume your itinerary.

Oaxaca shares the heritage of Indian ruins with the Yucatán. Entirely different tribes worked here, although at the same general time and with many similar techniques. The differences are in the detailing, which is specific to each tribe.

Oaxaca's two main attractions are ruins. Mitla, an exquisitely executed small retreat for dying or retiring Mixtec nobility, is in the hills twenty-four miles southeast of Oaxaca. Discovered on the site of a current day Indian village, Mitla is in remarkable condition and has not been restored. The Mixtec tribe took over as rulers of Monte Albán and the Oaxaca valley around 950 A.D. Whereas the Zapotecs used hieroglyphs on their structures, the Mixtec signature is symmetrical geometric designs in stone. At Mitla, entire walls are pieced together to form three-dimensional stone puzzles, using shadows to further elaborate the design. Interestingly, no human figures are portrayed here.

If the sharply angled stonework at Mitla is mind boggling, Monte Albán, just six miles up a curving road at the edge of Oaxaca, is six times as awe inspiring. Zapotecs, with some influence from the Olmecs, an earlier Indian tribe, leveled an entire mountaintop for this city. The work spanned seventeen centuries, and more than a dozen buildings still stand. The earliest of these are the observatory and "The Dancers," so named for the murals on its flat-faced rock slabs, each with a life-sized figure in a contorted pose. Our guide pointed out details that raise the possibility that the figures demonstrate illnesses and childbirth, and that the building may have been a hospital.

When the Mixtecs took over, they used the site as a burial ground. Beautifully crafted jewelry found there is now displayed at a museum in Oaxaca.

Each village in the area has a market day, and artisans bring goods to Oaxaca on Saturdays. As with many isolated areas of Mexico, each surrounding village has a speciality craft: leather goods, machetes and daggers, black pottery, hand-loomed cotton, carved idols, and dolls.

Beware this area's hard bargaining practices. I panicked when being browbeaten into buying excellent native wool dolls at Mitla and escaped to the tour bus. (The price came down just before the bus left.) Later we stopped at a small town market where women of the village massed at the entrance and picked off one wallet from our small group, even though we had been warned of such activity.

All in all, Oaxaca is a place I would like to stay for a week. You can stay that long and never see the same place twice, says one innkeeper. And unlike many parts of Mexico, the city offers activity, both native and commercial, most evenings.

Casa Colonial

The inngoers' haven in Oaxaca is Casa Colonial. Freshly painted aqua blue, this walled inn covers half a block and is within walking distance of the *zocalo* (main square). It is run by Mildred Madsen, an eighty-seven-year-old adventurous woman who spent most of her adult life in California on a valley ranch with her late husband. In 1973 the two of them leased this 1529 *hacienda* and enlarged it into an inn before he passed away and her vision faded. Now, as she shows guests around the grounds, it is hard to realize she has only peripheral vision. Never missing a step, she tours you through the living room, several bedrooms with baths, dining room, past the parrot named Segundo, and through the garden. Segundo? He or she is the second parrot in residence.

By then I had fallen for the room at the far right corner, in what had been part of a small chapel. Besides beautifully patterned tiled floors and high white walls and ceilings, it had Mildred's good old Middle America antiques, warmly colored spreads on the beds, and a walk-in shower. In her very positive way, though, Mildred decided we'd be happier in the next room.

The inn is often filled with groups that stay for two weeks, diligently studying the ancient Indian sites of Mitla and Monte Albán (see previous section). Various straw hats are arrayed by the door to protect these visitors from the nearly always present sun; and beautiful, historically accurate books on the sites are kept in the living room. Mildred herself has produced a modest book on some of the workers who made exciting discoveries at the Monte Albán site.

We stayed only two days, but Mildred had us tightly scheduled. After a prompt 7 P.M. supper, we walked to the *zocalo* to hear the music. Imagine seven men making wild music on three *marimbas*, with guitar and drum accompaniment, in a square crowded with joyful residents. No Anglos, no English. We loved it.

Breakfast was served exactly at 8 A.M.—all meals here are prompt and are signaled by the tinkle of a bell hanging outside the kitchen. No lagging for us. We were hustled off to Mitla and a few villages along the way, back by 2 P.M. for the day's main meal, and off to Monte Albán in the afternoon.

Tours are easy to arrange here, not only from large hotels, but also for pickup at Mildred's. A small bus stopped by at the appointed time, nearly filled with tourists staying elsewhere

Casa Colonial, Apartado 640, Calle Negrete 105, Oaxaca, Oax., Mexico. Telephone (operator assisted) 6-50-80. Or c/o Mary Hallock, 1315 Fourteenth Street, Santa Rosa, CA 95404. Telephone, evenings: 707-542-4094. Mrs. Mildred Madsen, hostess/owner. 12 rooms, most with private baths. Inexpensive; all meals included in price.

in the city. The driver was expecting us and asked us to convey his greetings to Mildred.

This lady has evidently put her own stamp on Oaxaca's current history—and, in a most pleasant maiden-aunt manner, on her guests. She likes them to dine with her to make sure no one spoils a vacation week with the runs. Breakfasts can be Mexican or North American: eggs *ranchería*, scrambled, soft-boiled, or other choices. The main meal is a full dinner with meat, starch, and vegetable; everyone gets the same dish. Supper is normally soup and bread, a culinary treat across the whole of Mexico.

Mildred longs for hot dogs, though. When she visits her daughter in California, she wants wieners for dinner—any style. She says you cannot eat hot dogs in Mexico, for ingredients may not be palatable.

Here's a smart lady talking. Do not eat hot dogs in Mexico.

During our night in Oaxaca, we were kept awake by what sounded like a chorus of birds, all singing the same note. Turns out the sounds were made by whistling lizards, who whistle only when rain is coming. Rain had been scarce the previous two years in this area, but it creates no particular problem when it comes. A big thundercloud pours out, usually for half an hour in the afternoon, then out comes the sun again.

There are three markets in Oaxaca and the big days are Saturdays and Sundays, which we missed. We did catch superaggressive hawkers of yarn dolls at Mitla ("Think of it as a game," extols a flyer for Casa Colonial) and a market in a nearby village where the women jam the entry and separate *gringos* from any loose wallets. Inside, gentlemen can buy some strange shredded bark said to make them more sexually profound, among other things.

Now what would a modern-day Alice in Wonderland make of that?

Hotel Victoria

I f you like your days out in the villages and ruins around Oaxaca but want your evenings a little more sophisticated than listening to whistling lizards and half a dozen *marimbas*, perhaps you should reserve a room at Hotel Victoria. While neither cozy nor ancient, the hotel appears to have been built in the 1930s, and its exterior is a rich peach stucco. Carved out of a hillside overlooking Oaxaca, it boasts impressive views from its dining room, bar, and most rooms. Yet it's only a five-minute, half-dollar taxi ride from town.

We arrived at Hotel Victoria after a personally conducted taxi tour of the city arranged by Mildred, owner of Casa Colonial (see previous entry). Her longtime gardener and inn manager enlisted an older son to zip us from one Oaxaca landmark to another before our plane left. In quick succession, we saw cathedrals, a prison, a medical center with marvelous life-sized statues of Mexican female dancers, and an overview of the city from higher up than Hotel Victoria, from where we could identify the sites we had visited.

This whirlwind tour was successfully completed with total dependence on our English–Spanish dictionary. Our most helpful, polite driver knew no English. But he knew what that book could do. We would look up, for instance, the phrase for "How old is the cathedral?" and hand the book to him; he would find the correct key words in English, experiment on pronouncing them, and return the book for the next communication.

The final exchange was something that amounted to "Take us to a large, cool *margarita*." He delivered us to Hotel Victoria.

There are fifty-six rooms, thirty-four bungalows and sixty junior suites here, but the hotel doesn't seem that big. Bungalows and wings are tucked out of sight among terraced gardens that cover the hillside. An array of squat and tall palm trees surround the Olympic-sized heated pool, and there are tennis courts.

I sat in the bar area, peering out over Oaxaca, enjoying a dollar *margarita*, and trying to pick out buildings from among the green mushrooms of trees covering the town section while waiting for the manager. A few cathedral steeples poked through the growth, but the town square, my point of reference, was heavily camouflaged. Dusk fell as the drink's glow took hold. Lights were turned on in the informal cafeteria-style restaurant. The menu posted at the entrance showed many à la carte choices, none over three dollars.

Finally, the manager was free. He led us up a circular staircase reaching to four stories from the entry lobby, a focal point of the hotel. One floor up, he opened the door to a typical junior suite, a lovely room with two double beds, sitting area, private bath, and view balcony. It was brightly furnished and well cared for.

I did not get to see the other three structures or single units so can just assume equal quality. The junior suites, roughly a dollar more than regular rooms, are the way to go. Although

Hotel Victoria, Apartado Postal 248, KM 545 Carretera Panamericana, Oaxaca, Mexico. Telephone (operator assisted) 951-6-26-33; telex 018-824. Fernando Martin del Campo, managing director. 151 rooms, bungalows, and suites. Inexpensive May–mid-December, moderate mid-December–April.

most rooms have view balconies, regular rooms are equipped with two single beds only—and what kind of romantic holiday would that be?

Even with all its modern amenities—a disco bar open nightly except Sundays, twenty-four-hour money exchange, television, and convention facilities—the atmosphere is warm and personal. The grounds are parklike, and the pool is an advantage. Hotel Victoria is not like the stainless-steel chain hotels, and yet travel agents may make your reservations here with comparative ease.

3

The Golden Triangle

I n the triangle that includes Mexico City, Cuernavaca, and Taxco, everything changed for the Indian tribes some 450 years ago. Aztecs conquered the Indian tribes that had built astonishing cities in eastern and central Mexico; then the Aztecs became victims themselves as Spanish invaders swept the country.

Hernán Cortés is the name that comes to mind when one considers Spanish invaders. Silver and gold were what he wanted, and he found these precious metals in Aztec coffers in Mexico City. He also found the raw product in Taxco's silver mines. For the next three centuries, until the early 1800s, when independence was won, Mexico's riches were shipped off to Spain.

Most intriguing to inngoers today are properties Cortés owned and developed and/ or gave to favorites of his. A number of them are now luxurious resorts in the Cuernavaca region. They are immense, as though Cortés wanted his own temples, as grand as those built for Indian leaders.

Mexico City, with a population of more than 13 million, fills a valley cupped by high mountains. All roads lead to the capital, which is near the center of the country, and all planes land there. Its 17,900-foot elevation keeps temperatures moderate. However, the surrounding mountains often hold factory and auto fumes stationary over the city, causing smog that can make you nauseous. It is a fascinating city if you can deal with the poverty, which is evident everywhere. My method of coping is to spend all day in the National Museum of Anthropology, an outstanding presentation of the country's heritage. This would be a perfect starting point for readers planning to visit some of the inns in this chapter.

Only one romantic Mexico City inn is described here. This is partly because I avoid the city whenever possible and partly because most of its guest rooms are in large high-rise hotels. My suggestion would be to stay in the city two nights, long enough to absorb the museum, and then rent a car or board a bus or plane, and head out.

If you can figure out how to get onto the freeway, it is possible to bypass Mexico City streets. The toll road leading south over the mountains and toward the Golden Triangle is at least two lanes in each direction, with easy curves and smooth grading. Tolls are only a few *pesos.*

Cuernavaca, first stop on the Golden Triangle, is a lovely colonial town of some 300,000 people. High walls hide most residences and gardens, but visitors can see the Borda Gardens and mansion, home of the imperial couple Maximilian and Carlotta in the 1860s. Also on view are the restored 1526 castle/fortress of Hernán Cortés, now a museum, and a still-functioning cathedral built in the same era.

It's only a short distance by toll road from here to Cocoyoc, site of a huge *hacienda* where Cortés had a sugar mill. The mill still stands on the grounds of a posh resort, and you can see remains of an overhead stone aqueduct.

Another short drive south brings you to yet another spread built for Cortés. Also a sugar plantation, this one is well fortified and carefully placed on a bluff over a river. This is the site of the present-day Hotel Hacienda Vista Hermosa.

To reach Taxco, which clings to ravines between the shoulders of mountains, you must depart the toll road and drive uphill via narrow, winding roads. Along the way you will see dark-shawled women carrying bundles and youngsters holding up deceased iguanas in hopes of a sale.

When we arrived in Taxco, a smiling young man waved us down, flashed his official guide identification, and volunteered to squeeze into the overflowing back seat of our rented Volkswagen to guide us to our destination. He gave us a city map and pointed out the location of the inn, but we did not hire him. Instead, we crept forward on the one-way street that squiggles and bobs horizontally toward the town's ancient cathedral and central plaza. Thinking we'd found the right vertical street—well, practically vertical—we turned left and found ourselves back on the highway. Didn't our spurned guide have a good laugh as we returned to the starting point again—twice! I must suggest hiring the guide, then parking the car and using taxis or your feet to get around town.

Hotel de Cortés

Talk about an oasis! In the smog-filled city of Mexico City, with its 13 million or more people and 13 million motor vehicles as well, this is it. Hotel de Cortés is situated near all the downtown government buildings, Alameda Park, and the recent diggings for ancient Aztec ruins. It is at the base of Paseo de la Reforma, the boulevard that leads through the Zona Rosa (shopping area) to the fabulous National Museum of Archeology. The hotel's stone face is squashed between shoe stores, magazine and book shops, and other meaner sights, such as mothers begging on the street corners.

But once you enter that 400-year-old gate of a former monastery, all the noise fades away. No fumes from buses and taxis intrude. The tranquil courtyard with fountain may be set with tables and chairs for dinner, or it may be readied for weekend fiesta dancing.

Your room, on one of two floors, is off a wide tiled arcade and furnished in heavy colonial style pieces. Window and door hardware must be from the days when monks used this as a base when they were sent from Spain to go out into the country and convert Indians to Christianity. Now, all rooms have private baths and telephones. Rooms look inward, to the patio, for views. Old trees and flowering bushes attract what birds there are near the center of Mexico City.

We stayed in a smaller room to the rear—very thankfully, for it was away from the street. Friends had a larger suite to the front, with sitting room space as well as bedroom. It was amazingly quiet, considering the tumult outside. But of course, the walls are solid rock, four feet thick.

Scattered around the rooms are many small unglazed ashtrays with a smiling Olmec-style face on one side, the hotel's name and location on the other. They practically say, "Take me home," which is why one is on my desk now.

The restaurant here is excellent, the staff attentive, polite, and knowledgeable of English. We thought if any place was safe to try the Mexican delicacy *ceviche* (raw fish cocktail), this would be it. Large plates were brought as a first course. A more gustatorily experienced traveling companion judged it excellent.

We spent quite a bit of time exploring on foot. The central *zocalo* is surrounded in part by the national palace, which was built by Cortés on the site of Moctezuma's palace. In its main stairwell is a two-story Diego Rivera mural of interest to patrons of the arts. More of his work is on view at Chapultepec Park.

The Alameda, directly across the street from Hotel de Cortés, has been a park since 1572. In early centuries, though, only the wealthy were admitted. Burnings at the stake took place here during the Holy Inquisition. The park, the largest one downtown, was entirely renovated in 1972.

Shopping and night life center around Zona Rosa, a quick taxi, bus, or subway ride down Paseo de la Reforma. To avoid disputes, make sure your taxi driver pushes the meter down before departing.

During our last day of sightseeing, the hotel's obliging staff stored our bags in a spare room even though we'd checked out. That seemed a thoughtful gesture for a big-city hotel. Surprisingly enough, this small hotel is part of the Best Western chain, and travel agents have no trouble making reservations.

Hotel de Cortés, Avenida Hidalgo 85, [Postal Code:] I Mexico City, D.F. Telephone (operator assisted) 905-85-0322; telex 017-77353, ATTEN BW DE CORTES. 27 rooms, all with private baths. Inexpensive except on holidays; moderate on holidays.

Las Mañanitas

In Spanish, "Las Mañanitas" is a birthday song, meaning "little mornings." To me, it means excellence in inn-keeping. A staff of 130 persons discreetly and smilingly tends to the needs of guests in fifteen rooms, the meticulous grounds, and of course, the most famous dining house in Cuernavaca. Seventh-generation royal crown African cranes prance over undulating lawns of a five-acre town estate. Here, too, dinner guests who have made reservations weeks ahead of time are served complimentary glasses of kahlua with their coffee.

A dozen bronze sculptures of Mexican women and children are spotlighted around the grounds. The waiters are sent to the best restaurants in Mexico City to learn the viewpoint of the customer. Here, everything in sight is scrubbed down every morning. No wonder the idle rich spend up to a month at a time.

Lord, one weekend was enough to spoil me.

This tranquil colonial house and grounds are near the heart of Cuernavaca, an hour's drive south from Mexico City. The entrance is an unassuming door in a wall along the street. So many unexpected delights are hidden by such plain looking walls, I'm tempted to knock on every door.

You are checked in quickly at the tiny lobby/bar and whisked through the house to open terraces at the rear, where meals and cocktails are served. Green umbrella-covered tables overlook well-tended lawns that slope downward, as toward a creek bed, under old palms and the biggest silk tree I've ever seen. Parrots and dozens of exotic long-legged birds parade by the fountain, as if for guests' benefit. Most noticeable are pure white peacocks and the African cranes, grey of body, with crests like those of today's teenagers and red circles on white cheeks.

Out of sight to the right is a full-sized swimming pool and

duck pond, more statuary, and lawns. To the left is the hotel's newer wing, which actually looks older. Four grand patio suites are in this long, one-story monastery-type structure, built with traditional materials and methods. But no self-sacrificing monk ever slept behind these carved wooden doors.

We were taken down a long, narrow hall, echoes bouncing off the stark white walls and flagstone floor. Behind the wooden door of our room was a whole living room with fireplace, an equally large bedroom, dressing room, Mexican tiled bath, and two patios. The high-ceilinged living room was separated, at least in feeling, from the next room by a huge rough-hewn crossbeam header supporting the bedrooms' traditional unglazed-tile-and-beam ceiling. A huge bed—which turned out to be two beds, hard enough for monks—sported a fine off-white spread, possibly hand-loomed linen. A carved wooden box hiding the tissues looks as though it's for ceremonial jewels. Heavy brass candlesticks, the kind you see in churches in Mexico, stand on the floor beside colonial Spanish dressers and side tables. Extra clothes storage space and closets are convenient for long visits.

The bath has matching tile sinks, and another sink and pull-up makeup table are in the dressing room, next to a smaller patio. The large patio, off the living room, lets you sit and enjoy the sun privately, behind high brick walls.

Tucked away in corners, rooms in the main house are less assuming but quite adequate and much less expensive. I'm sure any two travelers but the most picky could get along beautifully with the *hacienda's* mid-priced terrace suites, whose balconies overlook the gardens.

Built for an American woman in the 1930s, the *hacienda* was purchased in 1956 by Mrs. Margot Krause and her late husband, a lawyer from Oregon. They built the terrace suites and pool in 1960, the other wing more recently.

Candlelight dining here is an experience to be savored. Flickering shadows surround you, and bouquets of fresh flowers grace the white wrought iron tables. Evenings are balmy in Cuernavaca, normally temperate year round. The birds put on one last squawking contest before quieting down for the night.

Cranes are the logo here and are silhouetted on menus and china. The menu, written in Spanish and brought to the table on a large slate, is a collection of international favorites selected for guests from many parts of the world. Wanting to taste both their Continental and Spanish foods, we ordered standards of each: lentil soup and beef stroganoff, paired with *tortilla* soup and *chile relleno*. All were excellent, especially the stroganoff.

Breakfast, served to guests only, was filling and inexpensive but took forever. We used the time to watch the staff scrub down patio, furnishings, walkways, and fountains in view of the restaurant area—not where we were sitting, they had already done that—as the birds nosed around the freshly mowed lawns.

It was painful to pack our bags and prepare to drive to the next inn, sure it would be a letdown after the justly famous Las Mañanitas.

Las Mañanitas, Box 2201, Ricardo Linares 107, Cuernavaca, Morelos, Mexico. Telephone (operator assisted) 52-731-2-4646. Ruben Cerda, general manager; Margot Krause, owner. 14 rooms. Inexpensive, reasonable, and expensive.

Hotel Hacienda Cocoyoc

I t was nearly 11 P.M., time to retire in a huge canopied bed four pillows wide. I was staying in a magnificent luxury resort that was once a country estate of Hernán Cortés, ruler of all he surveyed.

All of a sudden I felt the floor move. Every rock of its hand-hewn frame shifted, sounding like a boxcar full of crabs. I was on the second floor of a 465-year-old stone hotel and there was an earthquake going on!

Actually, the wing where I got the shakes was built in 1978. Quakes seldom happen in the area, and this one was minor. "The hotel is still here," exclaimed the manager the next morning with a grin. Thank goodness, for this is one of the grandest and most historic of the properties once owned by the Spanish conqueror and now run as hotels. On the outer shoulders of the mountains that surround Mexico City, its magnificent ninety-six acres include a complex of hotel buildings that "would take an hour to walk around," laughed the desk manager when I asked for a tour. Within the tightly secured gates are buildings restored to their sixteenth-century grandeur. Overhead, an ancient stone aqueduct pours water into three huge bilevel pools. Gnarled roots of old trees twine around natural rock walls, forming works of art by Mother Nature. Mango groves shade a short golf course, tennis courts, and horse trails. There's a billiards room somewhere, and the centuries-old sugar mill is now a disco.

Actually, the history of this region predates Cortés. Legend has it that the Aztec king-god Quetzalcóatl was born close by. Later, Aztec emperors came here to rest.

Cortés built the *hacienda* in 1520. He then gave it to Emperor Moctezuma's daughter, Isabel Cortés Moctezuma, as a token of his passionate love for her. The sugar mill was built later, in 1613, by the Count of Monterrey. And Antonio de Mendoza, the first viceroy of New Spain, named it Hacienda Cocoyoc for the coyotes that still roam the hills to the north.

This breathtaking oasis, an hour south of Mexico City, was restored over seventeen years by Paulino Rivera Torres, a Mexican contractor. It now has 325 guest rooms, including twelve junior suites and twenty-four master suites with private wading pools. All are either air-conditioned or have ceiling fans, but the air at this altitude is usually around 72 degrees Fahrenheit.

Most weekend visitors are Mexican businessmen and their families, the manager said. And companies from other nations often book the technically up-to-date conference center, which is skillfully blended in with the grounds' other structures. Few people just wander in as we did. "Most guests stay a few days, escape the city noise and smog, get the sun, swim, then go on," explained Señor Rivas, desk manager.

That must be why there seemed to be less friendly communication between guests than at other inns we visited. One can wander around at will, people-watching, swimming, golfing without standing out as a foreigner. The urban businessmen and their wives don't speak to each other, much less to Anglos.

Hotel Hacienda Cocoyoc, Apartado 300, Cuautla, Morelos, Mexico. Telephone (operator assisted) 91-735-2-20-00. Señor Rivas, manager. *Reservations:* Padeo de la Reforma No. 308 1er. Piso 06600 Mexico D.F. Telephone 511-44-60; telex 1773564 COYOME. 300 rooms and suites. Inexpensive. Air-conditioning or fans.

Most of the 700-member staff know English, though, and are crisply polite.

We stayed in a junior suite off an open hallway complete with nesting sparrows and tropical gardens. The seven-foot-wide, six-foot-long bed had carved spindle posters and rust-colored fringe around the top. One sitting area and table were in front of a large arched window overlooking the landscaped courtyard; the other, with leatherette sofa and upholstered armchair, contained a television set. White stucco walls, twelve-foot ceilings, red tile floors with beige area rugs, and old wrought iron door hardware and locks follow the early Spanish style.

The beige and blue tiled bathroom was stocked with two bottles of carbonated water, oddly enough. Try brushing your teeth with that!

We dined in one of the hotel's five restaurants—the main one, actually—under high white arches. All tables were filled, and the noise from each table bounced off the walls like ping-pong balls, creating a general hubbub. It wasn't as annoying as it may sound, but we enjoyed our next breakfast and lunch at the poolside restaurant much more. The small outdoor tables are adorned with linens and fresh carnations. Whistling lizards sing up a storm louder than the splashing water from the aqueducts and swimmers. The menu includes everything from *tacos de pollo con guacamole* and *enchiladas rojas a verdes* to a club sandwich. The *margaritas?* Strong.

This lovely resort, with pink flamingos on the grounds and the largest parrots I've seen in its lobby, is just off a toll road to Mexico City, about ten miles east of Cuernavaca. Its mailing address, Cuautla, is deceiving, for it is in a small town named Cocoyoc.

Hotel Hacienda Vista Hermosa

A n interesting day's trip from either Cuernavaca or Taxco is Hacienda Vista Hermosa. Partway between the two, just off the toll road and hard to find without directions, this was once a sugar plantation, also built and owned by Cortés (see previous entry).

It seems the Spanish emperor Charles V awarded Cortés the title Marquis de Valle; 23,000 slaves and their villages; and lands now part of the states of Morelos, Mexico, Puebla, and Oaxaca. Cortés set many of his vassals to work constructing immense *haciendas* at Vista Hermosa. The whole complex was on a high bluff overlooking a riverbed, for Indians in that area were prone to attacking foreigners. Massive roofs and ceilings must have been for the same defensive purpose.

Before Cortés died, he had sugar cane planted and installed a factory to render syrup. The title, land, and *hacienda* were inherited by Cortés' son, Martín, who spent much of his time living it up at the Mexico City palace. Conspirators, angered at his excesses, met secretly at Hacienda Vista Hermosa, because of its distance from the capital, and planned his murder.

Their scheme failed and they were beheaded, but Martín was imprisoned and and later died in Madrid. Martín's grandson, Pedro, became Marquis de Valle and held the property until 1621. Part of it was then sold to friars. This and neighboring *haciendas* were later used to raise cattle.

During the revolution, Emiliano Zapata, champion of agricultural reform, led his followers on skirmishes in the region. Finally, when the battling was over, all of the 18,000-hectare property (one hectare equals 2.471 acres) was distributed among the people, except the ground under the *hacienda*. The building crumbled into ruin until its purchase and restoration by Fernando Martinez and Fernando Gonzalez. It took two years of removing rubble and replacing walls, doors, and tiles.

Entry from the main road is by a short rutted drive which passes squatters' sheds and discarded cars. The parking lot

Hacienda Vista Hermosa, Box 127, Cuernavaca, Morelos, Mexico. Telephone (operator assisted) Lada 91734-20-300; or Mexico City contact: 546-45-40. Nearly 100 rooms. Inexpensive.

and hotel facade are almost as depressing. No one was even in sight the day we arrived. But by walking through the main building, you come to a seemingly endless series of vaulted ceilings, corners balanced on pillars every eight to ten feet. I can't imagine the purpose of this, unless the only way to construct this pavilion-sized cloister was to support the heavy stone and plaster ceiling every few feet. At any rate, it is a breathtaking sight.

The colonnade faces a well-tended garden and walkway to other buildings. Following the path down a slight slope, we came to an ancient bullring with corrals for the animals and bleachers around the edge. The ring, no longer used, is on the bluff and provides views for miles.

Walking the other direction on the path, we peeked into another massive, nearly deserted building that had six-foot-thick walls and was honeycombed with stairways. The sugar syrup was kept cool here. Farther on, we passed a small disco area with nut husks on the dance floor, rounded a turn, and came to a large pavilion filled with dining tables and a few people. This was the hotel's dining room and adjoining bar. Beyond are nearly a hundred rooms and a large swimming pool with water splashing down from a stone aqueduct ages old.

We sat down at one of the linen-covered tables hoping to order a light lunch with our beer and were told no, it was a complete meal or nothing. So be prepared with either an empty stomach or a picnic to eat on the grounds.

By then we were ready to leave this dreary place anyway. I've included it only because two sources assured me it is a favorite of Mexico City businessmen and really hums on weekends. To me, though, there is something evil lurking about the place, even today.

Hacienda del Solar

Y ou lie, propped up by pillows, on a firm (not hard) *real* king-sized bed. Mexican tiles, swirls of mustard and orange, cover the floor to a wrought iron railing and down a few steps to an open sitting area the width of the bedroom. The walls are stark white, accentuating dark carved furniture and works of art such as a life-sized wood carving of St. Francis of Assisi.

Gazing over the top of the sitting area, out the twelve-by six-foot sliding glass doors and past a private patio as large as the sitting room, you look across miles and miles of uninhabited sawtooth crags, dropping away ever so gradually from the mountain town of Taxco. Above, clumps of clouds billow upward into the clean blue sky like so many melting baked Alaskas. Mornings you are above the cloud layer, crags hidden from view.

This is one of twenty-four rooms and suites at Hacienda del Solar. It's better than any Hilton penthouse. And with a five-star restaurant on the grounds and meals included in the amazingly low room charge, you feel like king or queen of the mountain. Sixty acres of grounds cap a hill above a silver mine, the largest of the seven mines still being worked here. Taxco, two hours south of Mexico City, was famous for the metal, even before Cortés' time.

The *hacienda* is comparatively new in Mexican terms. The first building was adapted into a home by Ted Wick, West Coast director of publicity for CBS in the 1950s and one-time agent for singer Nancy Sinatra. It was sold a few times before purchase by Claire and Sam Polk of Mount Vernon, New York. By then the large pool and some other buildings had also been installed. The Polks used these for extended holidays and guests' quarters, and in 1973 they made Wick's home into the restaurant

La Ventana de Taxco. People began asking for rooms, so the next phase followed in 1978. Just this past winter, two more suites with kitchens were added.

On the other side of the hill from the housing quarters, the restaurant's view is of the picturesque town of Taxco, which tenaciously clings to the mountainside a few miles away. Tables for a few dozen diners are along a ten-foot-wide corridor with floor-to-ceiling sliding glass on three sides. Cocktails are served in two adjoining areas which resemble comfortable living rooms. Ted Wick returns weekend evenings to play popular medleys on the piano—"My piano," he declares proudly. He sold it with the house but enjoys playing once or twice a week.

Mario Cavagna of Como, Italy, runs the restaurant, and it is a jewel. From the hummingbird logo stamped in the brass plate at each place setting, to the salad, tossed by a crew of three waiters, to the green-and-white color scheme in the china, table linens, and staff clothing, everything is elegant. Even the breakfast cream—for cereal and coffee—was served in a pitcher instead of a straight-edged water glass as is the custom in this strange but beautiful country.

The lasagna I ordered came to the table shaped as a half pineapple, with freshly made pasta, leaves of radish, and curling chives as wide as celery. My companion's choice, a chicken in chocolate sauce (*molé*) was just as beautifully presented.

The lower floor of this building contains a common room—a

Hacienda del Solar, Apartado Postal 96, Taxco, Guerrero, Mexico. Telephone (operator assisted) 732-2-03-23. Isabel Carbajal, hostess; Samuel Polk, owner. 24 rooms including 4 suites. Moderate; price includes breakfast and one other meal.

sort of library-sitting room—and half a dozen regular rooms. These quarters, as well furnished as the junior suite, are quite large enough for extended stays, and their sitting areas share the restaurant's view.

In the library, I found a shelf of New York Social Registers through 1968. Polk is included along with the other potentates, and his occupation is listed as business and holiday gift sales. He comes to Taxco a month at a time, several times a year.

To reach the main part of the hacienda, you cross the restaurant's open patio and climb steps up and over an entry road. This brings you to just below the crest of the hill; a path winds around the peak. To the left is a wide half-lap pool, deck, tennis court, and vine-covered corner bar area that offers drinks and light refreshments. Oleander, bougainvillea, and metal sculptures surround the lawn.

If the chaise longues look a little scruffy, it's because of Tigré. Tigré is a huge, friendly short-haired dog. The first time we stopped here, he greeted guests on arrival. Now he's retired to poolside. When guests come to swim, he climbs down from one chaise longue, greets them, then climbs up on another to continue his snooze.

The entrance to "Annette," our abode in the hacienda, was down natural steps in the hill to a carved wooden door in the rock wall at the end of the house. Chinked between the large stones, by the way, are little shards—an old masonry technique. Inside to the right, behind another locally carved door, is a bath with hand-painted tiles to the ceiling. Matching tiles line a sink, counter, the sunken tub (large enough for two), and the sunken garden behind a full-length opaque window. Everything works. No chips or dings. You are, however, advised to use purified water from a jug.

To the left is the spacious bedroom with spindle-type headboard and a woven spread, striped with the warm colors of Mexico, which covers the oversized bed. All the dressers, end tables, and other furniture are well-executed local products.

Below a wrought-iron rail, the sitting room, half as large, holds one of those hide-covered table-and-chair sets as well as a loveseat facing the view. Or, you can sit at the table on the brick patio, or in the chaise longues. For cold nights, use the small brick-lined fireplace and pull the big louvered doors across the glass—if you can bear to shut out the view.

It is indeed hard to comprehend that all this luxury—which includes two meals—is yours at the price of a room in a first-class U.S. hotel.

Hotel Santa Prisca

A block up the hill from Taxco's main plaza is Hotel Santa Prisca, a two-story, white stucco rectangle surrounding a lovely garden and tinkling fountain. Rooms here have excellent ventilation: The entry side faces the garden, the other an arched window overlooking the town. All have private baths and are simply but adequately furnished. Inquire about beds if you want to be sure of a double, for the rooms I saw had twins, Mexican style. And be sure to ask for a room with a view, for not all are so blessed.

The hotel also boasts six junior suites "with private bath and watering pot, hot and cold water every time," as their brochure puts it. You can reserve here under the European plan (without meals) or with breakfast included at $5 or $6 extra. The restaurant, in a long tiled walkway surrounded by arched windows and doorways, serves international and Mexican dishes. White cloths and gaily colored china dress tables with simple ladderback chairs. Lighting is from star-shaped leaded glass fixtures. The small plant-surrounded bar is called La Jaula ("the cage").

You can spend quiet afternoons on the garden paths or in the small library, dedicated to the memory of a former guest. I prefer to climb up to the roof, where a wide, open area is dotted with patio furniture. Beyond the red tile railing, the whole town of Taxco spreads out before you. Prominent in the foreground is Santa Prisca Cathedral, heart of Taxco, along with the town square it faces. Beyond the church, the shops, and crazy crooked streets, mountains and valleys surround the busy hamlet.

This hotel makes a good base for exploring the town. Right out front is one of the town's public wells, where townspeople seem to gather just as statesiders congregate at the laundromat or post office. The well is also the center of a rare flat spot on the hillside, which autos often use as a turnaround.

On festival days, of which there are many in Mexico, the action centers one block down the hill, at the central square. We watched costumed high-school-aged children perform traditional dances there one afternoon; perhaps five hundred other spectators stood around the tile-paved *zocalo*. I must admit, part of the time we watched from a second-floor open bar overlooking the square, the better to see over the heads of other observers. An evening visit to the same bar found a rather inebriated resident verbally fighting the battle of the

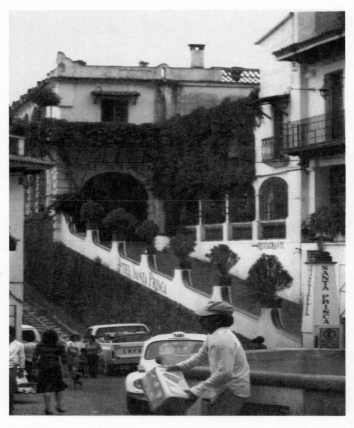

Hotel Santa Prisca, Cena Obscuras No. I, Apartado Postal No. 42, Taxco, Guerrero, Mexico. Telephone (operator assisted) 732-2-00-80 or 732-2-09-80. 38 rooms on 2 floors (ask for view room). Inexpensive (under $25). Marcelina Estrada, reservations.

Alamo all over again, luckily with other *gringo* tourists.

Interesting silver shops and other establishments line the square and the tilted block back up to Santa Prisca. Handcrafted silver jewelry, usually sold by the ounce, is a good buy. Shop owners are proud of their craftsmanship. At one, we were shown the prize-winner of the previous silver fair, an ornate sailing ship, all in silver.

Taxco is not known as the place to buy cotton blouses and dresses, but I have twice found what I wanted, for the best of prices, at a second-floor factory salesroom near the upstairs bar on the plaza.

Shopping and sightseeing in Taxco is best done on foot. One nice feature about Hotel Santa Prisca is its secure parking lot. In a town with narrow, twisting, one-way streets, it is a relief to park the auto and walk.

4

The Colonial Circle

erhaps the best-known area of central Mexico—at least by natives of the United States—is the Colonial Circle's great agricultural valley, edged with mountains and north of Mexico City. Its picturesque colonial towns contain Gothic churches and opera houses, universities and bullrings, and of course markets where craftspeople from the countryside sell wares next to live chickens and beautiful produce.

San Miguel de Allende may have a familiar ring, for North American art students and writers by the hundreds have attended a semester or two at Instituto Allende, an accredited school of fine arts. A number now maintain homes there, forming the nucleus of a large English-speaking population. This may help explain why the local art, which is on display everywhere—even in a fast-food lunch counter we found—is more subdued in color and sophisticated in style than elsewhere in the country.

San Miguel is an old town, founded in 1542 by a friar of that name. The Allende (ay-YEN-day) was added later to honor Ignacio Allende, a revolutionary hero who was born there. Today, the whole town is a historic zone, and any construction must be approved as fitting. The names of its ancient houses and narrow, crooked streets, which change names every few blocks, are in no way Anglicized; fortunately, nearly all residents understand English.

Guanajuato (whan-ah-WHAT-o) is, or was, a silver town, and it is somewhat similar to Taxco. Less steep and at a lower altitude, it still sports narrow, winding streets that network over several shoulders of lush, rolling hills. One underground street follows a long-deserted mine tunnel.

Once prosperous, the city is still attractive and small enough for exploring by foot. An impeccably uniformed policeman with a musical two-tone whistle directs traffic at the town's center and flowers fill the old silver mine carts along the main street. Also on this street are the University of Guanajuato; a gem of a colonial theater, fully restored; and an enclosed market in a magnificent ironwork building the size of a football field. Scrolls and peaks of iron embellish the outside of the market. Inside, the main floor is devoted principally to foodstuff. Stalls on the railed mezzanine, around all four walls, feature clothing, shoes, dishes, and knickknacks. Neither price regulation nor unnerving bargaining operate here. If you don't like the deal at one booth, move on to the next.

Among Guanajuato's other sights are a statue honoring Pipila, a miner who braved loyalists' bullets to set fire to their stronghold; and a display of well-preserved mummies, which we decided to miss.

Down on the fertile valley floor, Querétaro (cah-RAY-tah-ro) is said to have been a townsite before the coming of the Spanish. It was here that secret meetings of rebel forces took place in the 1790s, and where Mexico signed the treaty that gave the United States lands north of the Rio Grande.

Farther south, toward Mexico City but within the state of Querétaro, is San Juan del Rio, where we discovered two inns. The land under them, historians say, was owned by Cortés, who in 1546 built a grand *hacienda* there for his interpreter and mistress, La Malinche. Boasting 9,000 head of cattle and 2,000 horses, it came to be the region's richest and most important agricultural operation.

Later, bulls for the ring were raised here. In 1940 the land was divided, and much stone from the *hacienda* was removed to build private homes in the area.

This part of the Colonial Circle encompasses the major agricultural support system for Central Mexico. Its constant springlike weather and wide valleys provide a long vegetable and fruit growing season. Large plots in the high valleys are tilled by machine; small hillside farms by oxen, horse, or burro. As with the rest of Mexico, no useful piece of land is left idle.

The rest of the Colonial Circle is to the west, on the way to Guadalajara.

La Mansión Galindo

One reason your interest rarely wanes in Mexico is you never know what to expect—such as a grand mansion of a hotel in the midst of rich agricultural flatlands nearly two hundred miles north of Mexico City and forty south of Querétaro, a service center for the area.

Motoring north in quest of inns, we found La Mansión Galindo quite by accident. It was among our most exciting discoveries.

We were staying at Hacienda La Mansión, a few miles beyond the end of the toll road, near the village of San Juan del Rio; after arriving, we had learned about its sister hotel. So the next day, we drove down a well-paved, arrow-straight road through small fields owned by Mexican farmers but once part of a 60,000-acre estate owned by Cortés.

Remains of the *hacienda's* central stone buildings lay abandoned for thirty-five years after Mexico's land reform before entrepreneur Piero Ricci purchased the site in 1975 for restoration as a luxury hotel and conference center designed by Xavier Barbosa. After a few years as a Hyatt Hotels property, it is now in the hands of Groupo Visa Tourisma.

The results of the restoration are stunning. You drive down a wide, neatly kept cobblestone lane past some of the newer stone houses to a courtyard set amid several massive stone buildings. It's hard to tell which one the hotel lobby is in, since all are equally dominant. A gardener pointed the way for us.

Walking inside is akin to stepping into a Spanish lord's home. The lobby is furnished with antiques and magnificently large oil paintings that look as though they belong in a museum. Surrounded by such elegance, you feel you should bow or curtsy before the first passerby.

Yes, the manager would show us a few rooms. He led us

along carpeted hallways eighteen feet wide with seating areas along the way, and up a full-width stairway to a room with old wooden double doors enhanced by rich brass hardware. Beyond the foyer was the carpeted living room, as large as that of the average home, with upholstered pieces, a television, a dining set, and a small pay-as-you-use refrigerator. The windows opened onto acres of beautifully maintained gardens.

The bedroom beyond contained two double beds and another television set. Fresh flowers and rich oil paintings adorned both the bedroom and living room.

The bathroom had an enclosed commode and enclosed tub/shower, so both could be used simultaneously with privacy. A little basket is set out with shampoo, soap, and, believe it

La Mansión Galindo, Apartado 16, San Juan Del Rio 76800, Querétaro, Mexico. Telephone (operator assisted) 91-467-20050; telex 12804 HLMAME. Miguel Angel, Rodriguez Galvain, managers. 166 rooms and suites. Moderate and expensive.

or not, washcloths (a rarity in Mexico). Bottled water is also provided.

We were shown a slightly larger suite on the main floor. An outdoor spa bubbled in the patio off the living room. The bedroom, with king bed, had a separate patio. This was one of two top-of-the-line suites, but of the 157 rooms and nine suites, seventeen have private spas and terraces.

Like the hallways, the public rooms are on a grand scale, with towering ceilings and dark, carved furnishings. Especially nice is a formal brick patio, rectangular in shape and completely surrounded by a wide arcade whose arches rest on old pockmarked columns. On the far side, the convention center has been fashioned from original barns with majestic arches and elevated ceilings.

It would be fascinating to stay a few days and try to figure out what other parts of the hotel once housed.

We stopped for breakfast in one of the dining rooms whose arched French doors open onto this courtyard. After ordering, I noticed that one of the sets of doors was not real, but painted. In fact, the whole room was painted to give the effect of sitting in a lattice-enclosed garden room. Clouds dot a blue sky twenty feet above. On the interior wall, a painted door is ajar and a Latin couple, she with a black lace *mantilla*, peek out to see who is dining. The mural was done by an English artist, John Beadle, who lives in San Miguel de Allende.

As we sat at the linen-covered table in wooden armchairs covered in black leather, two jams and some hot red sauce were brought to the table, along with both buttered toast and sliced Mexican bread. My order of *tortilla ranchero* turned out to be a perfectly round concoction of eggs, *chorizo*, potatoes, onion, and chili, delicately browned on both sides, plump as a donut, and served with refried beans. I must say, this was the most elegantly prepared and served breakfast we found.

La Mansión Galindo has tennis courts, pools, a golf course, nightly entertainment, and a ballroom that holds 800 people. Best of all, it offers a grand atmosphere, full of mystery from the past, and the finest modern conveniences.

Hacienda La Mansión

A s mentioned, we stopped at this hotel before inspecting La Mansión Galindo. We had learned that it was a historic building, but that's using the term loosely. It was a warehouse for the meats, grains, and other ranch supplies used at the nearby Hacienda Galindo. A portion of the building still stands, holding public rooms with old-style ceiling construction. Large glazed tiles cover the floor under black and tan striped carpet. That plus a large open fire give the small bar and restaurant an intimate air.

A convention of businessmen from Mexico City had already filled most of the crowded dining room, so we waited in the bar for a table. La Mansión does not stock expensive bourbons and scotches, thereby eliminating complaints about prices. But favorite Mexican beverages are in full supply.

Waiters in the bar and restaurant speak English, and the menu is bilingual. Steaks, chicken, and fish are offered, as well as Mexican specialties. The dining room is pleasant, with many windows overlooking the patio, swimming pool, and, to the back of the property, ancient pepper trees. Table linens take a cue from the garden, with green cloths over white skirts, white napkins folded over like fans, and bright red carnations in vases. As dusk changed to dark, subdued lights behind mantles of yellow glass became apparent.

I had become leery of ordering beef in Mexico but was pleasantly surprised by a tender, medium-rare rib-eye steak. It was served with two vegetables on china bearing the hotel's logo. To the side, a few bougainvillea blossoms added a decorative touch. This, the soup, and a creamy mango mousse were excellent. The bread, containing a bit of unidentifiable spice, was irresistible. The only letdown was a raw white wine selected from the display on a central table. Living in California's wine country does prejudice one.

Our room at this hotel, a junior suite, was across the gardens from the dining room in a modern one-story wing. Built of brick, the hotel is only twenty years old.

Opening off a long, wide hallway, suites are arranged rail-road-flat style, with a two-room bathroom just off the entry, a fairly large bedroom and, at the far end, a formal library behind heavy paneled double doors. Walls are whitewashed brick except for the bright orange wall behind the king-sized bed. Other color spots are a few framed Indian paintings and the warm, multicolored bedspread and matching window curtains. The bedroom also has a nice seating area with hide armchairs and a brick windowseat by a round table.

But the intriguing part is the library, or sitting room. One could have a secret rendezvous there and no one would be the wiser. Even someone at the suite door would find it impossible to tell what might be going on behind the closed doors of the library. Even more intriguing, our key did not work in the lock of the small metal door between the library and the garden. Outside, this entry is practically hidden by overgrown bushes.

This suite had electric heat, a telephone, and television. Isn't it fun to watch a news broadcast in Spanish? Other con-veniences include two luggage stands; well-vacuumed black and tan striped carpet throughout, including the bath; a bilin-gual questionnaire about hotel service; tissues; a built-in ashtray by the commode, and a built-in ceramic seat in the shower.

We slept well that night in the comfortable, three-pillow-wide bed. The only problem is that the hotel is so close to the highway that you can't ignore the noisy trucks and buses. On the other hand, Hacienda La Mansión has its own gas station— a definite plus, for there aren't any between the outskirts of Mexico City and the end of the toll road that brings you here.

Hacienda La Mansión, Apartado Postal 16, San Juan del Rio, Querétaro, Mexico. Telephone (operator assisted) 91-467-2-01-20. 108 rooms and suites. Inexpensive.

Casa de Sierra Nevada

Near the center of the lively town of San Miguel is Casa de Sierra Nevada, a posh though extremely reasonable eighteen-room inn occupying three homes of Calle de Hospicio. Curiously enough, *hospicio* meant originally "shelter" or "lodging for travelers." The inn is hard to find, however, for the street soon twists and changes its name.

At the heart of the Casa de Sierra Nevada is a 300-year-old villa where the archbishop of the cathedral around the corner once resided. Later it housed guests of a marquis of Sierra Nevada, whereby its name. In the past six years, the villa was restored, the other two houses purchased, and all were converted to inn use. Then, in the winter of 1981, a group headed by Peter Oscar Wirth purchased the property. Peter is Swiss, grew up in Italy, speaks five languages, and represents the fifth generation of his family in the hotel business. He is proud of the fact that Sierra Nevada is the only Mexican member of Relais et Châteaux, a prestigious worldwide association of hostelries. Nonetheless, Peter charges less than others in the association because he feels he can't give luxury service here; there are no schools to train staff. Besides, the government establishes his prices.

The rooms have been left much as they were, so a stay here feels like visiting a Mexican villa. Of course, this means that some are much nicer than others, and sources say to request rooms other than in the main villa.

Ours was Suite 8, on the first floor of a house across the way. Its dimensions, twenty-seven by eighteen feet, are grand; it must have been the formal living room. A full fireplace with six-foot-long mantle faces the street window and a sitting area with seven-foot sofa, loveseat, conversation chairs, and a five-foot-long desk. Above, an eighteen-candle brass candelabrum is suspended from a mushroom-shaped cupola five feet across and with little round windows.

A heavy screen defines the bedroom area, furnished with a similarly heavy armoire for clothing and hard twin beds, a Mexican proclivity. Electric blankets and floor heater were provided but not needed. The tiled bath is the width of the

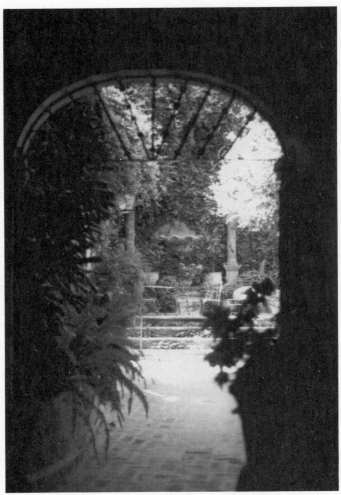

Casa de Sierra Nevada, Hospicio 35, San Miguel de Allende, Guanajuato, Mexico, 37700. Telephone (operator assisted) 52-465-2-04-15. Peter Wirth, manager. 19 rooms and suites. Inexpensive and moderate.

room, and a four-by five-foot mirror reaches partway up to the high ceiling.

At least one of four cheery maids was always available. All understand English, reply to you in Spanish, then repeat key words in English to be sure all is understood.

Meanwhile, the room was enough to start us dreaming of running out to the street and inviting twenty-five people to a cocktail party just so we could show it off. Instead, we dressed for dinner and stopped by the English-pub-style bar in the archbishop's former quarters. The formality of European armchairs, prints of old world maps, ships, and samplers contrasts greatly with the adjoining courtyard, where we felt more at home with *margaritas* and hors d'oeuvres. A *tejamanil* ceiling of thin wood strips covers the patio and restaurant. Similar to the diagonal strip paneling in today's modern homes, this style is no longer allowed in Mexico as the country is conserving wood.

Throughout the hotel, you can't turn around without viewing excellent paintings, ceramics, sculpture, and textiles. This is true of the entire town of San Miguel, long an art center.

The excellent dining facilities comprise several small rooms strung together. Peter takes advantage of this by separating his international guests from the sometimes raucous locals. Our dinner for two, including salads and a filet mignon, was an amazing $12. Delicious, too. In a country where beef is often tough, Peter sends his van to a particular butcher in a town ninety minutes away for properly aged meats. Another favorite of guests is chicken curry. And if imported wine from the well-stocked cellar tempts you, consider the price: It costs more than the food.

Next morning, a single generous room-service Continental breakfast was under $4. Don't bother with dining room breakfast, for the service can be exasperatingly slow.

Casa de Sierra Nevada is a satisfying experience, mostly because of Peter's attention to detail, his training of the staff, and his being on the premises. Peter, his young wife, and their baby girl Sabrina live in a fourth house on the same street.

Hotel Villa Jacaranda

H otel Villa Jacaranda, a few blocks away from Casa de Sierra Nevada, is housed in a former mansion. Owner Don Fenton is from Seattle, one of thousands who can say they were former Boeing employees. He found San Miguel de Allende and fell in love with it and with his wife, a native of this town.

Ten years ago they started their inn/restaurant. Don, who seems the sort who would be unhappy sitting still, added a room here, a bath there, until they had accommodations for a dozen couples. Or maybe fourteen by now. When we visited, he was tearing out old lumber to make room for a bar and had recently purchased the lot next door for future expansion.

Rooms and suites here tend to be light and airy, some having skylights. Hand-carved and painted screens define living areas in the comfortably large rooms, where works by local artists are displayed. White wrought iron tables and chairs furnish the sitting areas, and fireplaces take the edge off the few chilly nights. In some suites, the bedroom is upstairs. In others, arches divide the space between bedroom and sitting area. All have private or semiprivate patios with seating. The double beds are delightfully soft for Mexico. Although bedroom and sitting area are covered with soft beige carpets, tiles in the private baths were made in nearby Dolores Hidalgo, well known for this craft, and basins match the wall patterns.

The gardens here are on several levels and a jumble of flowering plants and bushes edge the patios. Flowers also surround the dining room's exterior seating.

The restaurant, a Travel-Holiday award winner since 1980, is Don's pride, for he is the chef. Half the tables are in the main floor of the house, half outside on a poolside patio. We chose the latter and sat at a white wrought iron table near a

Roman plunge, or small, shallow pool. From a nicely varied menu of Mexican, American, and international choices, we picked soup and sandwich on a cheese board, which was satisfying and well presented, and a delicious seafood crêpe with lobster, served with just-cooked asparagus. Don claims the mild weather thereabouts produces an eight-month asparagus and strawberry season. Eat your hearts out, nouveau cuisine chefs of the United States. With year-round daytime temperatures from 75 to 85 degrees and its 6,000-foot elevation, San Miguel de Allende is not too shabby for human beings, either.

Don likes to prepare classics, such as gazpacho and baked stuffed shrimp, along with his own creations. Most tend to be light, like the fresh local products now featured in the States. This sets Don apart, for one can find refried beans and rice half a block in any direction in most of Mexico.

Don's wife and growing family also work at the inn. His son took bags in for guests the day we visited. Although there is no minimum stay at Villa Jacaranda, many guests stay up to three months at a time. Many more arrive by train for a five-or seven-day package excursion that starts in Nuevo Laredo, just across the border from Laredo, Texas. You leave your car at a lot on the Texas side, taxi across the bridge, and board the

Hotel Villa Jacaranda, Aldama 53, San Miguel de Allende, Guanajuato, Mexico 37700. Telephone (operator assisted) 52-465-2-10-15. Gloria and Don Fenton, owners. 12 rooms and suites. Inexpensive.

Aztec Eagle for Mexico City at 6:55 P.M. Bring a basket picnic and cooler—the train has no dining service—and reserve a private compartment. You arrive at San Miguel fresh and ready to go at 1:10 the next afternoon.

This package would be especially attractive for those who do not want to drive in Mexico, for a car is not needed in San Miguel and taxis are inexpensive if you want to wander. Quite a few Texas drawls were heard around the pool that day, but the adventure could of course start by car or plane from anywhere in the States. The overnight return trip leaves San Miguel at 2:30 P.M. for an early morning arrival at the border.

Villa Santa Monica

I n a quieter setting, across the town's lily-scented French Park and on a larger gardened plot, is Villa Santa Monica. Its Texan owner, Betty Kempe, was out of town, so an assistant manager showed us around the eight-room inn whose cheery rooms with bright Mexican rugs and spreads look out on well-tended grounds terraced down to a stream. In the other direction, through screened, arched doors, the rooms open on to a flower-and bird-filled patio with the familiar fountain as its centerpiece. The birds are wild except for Far Out, the resident parrot.

One room near the entrance especially caught my eye. A cozy sitting room with a small fireplace and a tiled bathroom with a sunken tub are downstairs; and an equally cozy bedroom loft, not much bigger than the double bed, is upstairs behind a rail.

On registering, you are given a large brass room number with three keys attached: to your room, the front door, and the garden gate. The latter two are locked at night. A wide covered breezeway surrounds the central courtyard, and the stretch nearest the entry forms the open-ended living room. An over-sized stone fireplace, sink-in sofas, coffeetables, and books make this a comfortable, informal spot.

Farther along the breezeway is an honor-system bar from which complimentary *tequila* sours are served at 6:45, before dinner. At other times, you serve yourself and sign for beverages.

Meals are served on the main patio, weather permitting. This area seats thirty, so guests can entertain new-found friends here, except on Sundays, when the restaurant is closed.

Elena has been the hotel's cook ever since Betty Kempe opened the villa. Betty hired a French chef to train her, so Elena's skills include Continental favorites. One supper a week is traditional Mexican food, but other nights vary. Elena shops in the morning at the *mercado*, or market, for whatever looks fresh; that determines the evening meal, which is the same for everyone. Herbs, vegetables, and fruits come from the inn's garden, as do homemade jams and chutney. Breakfasts provide many choices and can be as *gringo* or Mexican as you like.

The inn's grounds and gardens—both floral and vegetable—are visual delights, but just across the street lies a large park where pink lilies bloom for three consecutive months. Known formally as Juarez Park and informally as French Park, it is ideal for strolling or resting on benches. Don't be surprised if you hear squawking in the trees as you walk along the landscaped terrain. White egrets have made their homes here, and they usually perch precariously in overhead branches.

Perhaps other birds perched and watched as Villa Santa Monica was being built at the end of the eighteenth century by the Conde de Baeza, a wealthy silver miner from Guanajuato. After the revolution, the house remained empty for nearly a century, until the 1930s, when Mexican film and opera star José Mojica restored it to elegance. Among his many famous guests at the villa, Dolores del Rio and Ramon Navarro even planted

Villa Santa Monica, Baiza 22, Apartado 134, San Miguel de Allende, Guanajuato, Mexico, 37700. Telephone (operator assisted) 52-465-2-09-14; -2-15-93; and -2-09-98. Betty Kempe, owner; Natalie Spencer, manager. 8 rooms. Moderate; meals included.

a tree in the garden, now commemorated by a plaque. Then, when Mojica's adored mother died a few years later, he gave away all his worldly goods, moved to Peru, and became a Franciscan friar.

The villa changed owners several times between then and 1970, when Betty converted it into a guesthouse. For a short period, she rented it as a time-share vacation facility; now it's an inn again.

Betty and her manager, Natalie Spencer, have been innkeeping for some time. One sure sign of this is a simple flyer given to guests at check-in time, entitled "Questions Most Frequently Asked." It includes a brief history of the house, pertinent information about parking, keys, meals, the bar, laundry service (included in the price), phone, mail, the dry sauna and tiny swimming pool, taxi service, and even how to recover from Moctezuma's revenge, if you should suffer from it. They must save hours of time with this printed message.

The daily rate, around $70, covers two people for room, all meals, tips, and laundry.

Hotel Castillo Santa Cecilia

I f there could be a Mexican counterpart to California's over-
stated Madonna Inn of San Louis Obispo, this is it. Visits
to both the 100-room California creation of Alex Madonna
and to Hotel Castillo Santa Cecilia are rewarding, one-of-a-
kind experiences.

Built in the late 1950s on the grounds of a tiny chapel on
a hill above Guanajuato (whan-ah-WHAH-toe), it has every indi-
cation of being an ancient Spanish-style castle. Travel guides
often credit it with being much older. Perhaps it's because the
date 1860 is emblazoned on the shower curtains. Perhaps that's
when the chapel was built—it certainly doesn't refer to the
hotel's establishment.

Still, what a fun place to stay when visiting the pleasing
little mining town high in the mountains, about a five-hour
drive north of Mexico City. The castlelike Castilla Santa Cecilia
lies just out of sight but within walking distance of the bustle
of shops (walk down, but taxi back up to the hotel). Edged
with brick, its grey stone face extends four stories, more or
less, to corner turrets with peepholes. I say "more or less"
because the building is like a rabbit warren, erected on the
hillside's assorted levels and with arched hallways going this
way and that.

You enter the grounds through a massive stone arch. Inside,
all you can see are heavy, large-scale grey stone structures
closing in. The turreted main building is across a small courtyard from the tower-topped main restaurant, and walls ring the
lower edge of the slanted property. If it wasn't on such a hilly
site, there would probably be a moat outside the walls.

By the central fountain is the check-in lobby for the eighty-eight rooms, seven junior suites, and one master suite. Our junior suite, suite B, was just a short distance down a tiled hall past simulated wall torches. Tiles here are large black squares spaced with equally large white blocks, 1940s style.

The junior suite itself is like a warren: arches to the left, arches to the right, arches overhead—eight in all. Each room, including the bath, has a rough brick ceiling, bowed up, with a brick-ringed skylight at its peak. Dark wooden arched doors close off each segment of this suite: the entry, with a round table and chairs for four; a bedroom with twin beds; another bedroom with a king-sized bed; the bath; and a closet-sized room with no apparent function. That's right, two complete bedrooms. And if that's not enough, arched alcoves adjoin the bedrooms, with waist-high arched windows fitted with dia-mond-shaped leaded glass. The city and mountains beyond provide a great view.

There are no wall hangings, so the eye returns to the curves of the ceiling, accentuated at night by small spotlights and an elaborate glass and brass light fixture by the bed. The cut glass casts diamond-shaped patterns around the room. Spread with heavy embroidered fabric, the same rich material used in a

Hotel Castillo Santa Cecilia, Apartado Postal 44, Guanajuato, Gto., Mexico. Telephone (operator-assisted) 2-04-85 or 2-04-77; in U.S., (800) 221-6509; telex 12326 CASTME. Javier Mendoza, manager. 88 large rooms. Inexpensive.

tassle-edged half canopy, the bed is comfortably soft, with feather pillows and a white mattress skirt.

The rooms are large, furnished with heavy spindle-design desks and dressers. Telephones, televisions, and one of those pay-for-what-you-eat refrigerators are supplied.

Wow!

The round main restaurant is also Moorish and like a castle. Arches separate outer tables from inner ones, and a round buffet is in the exact center under a double-tiered candelabrum that resembles a candle-dipping wheel and whose lights look like candles. Here and there, crested banners hang from the ceiling. Subdued, regal sounding music plays in the background.

Although there is a menu, you are encouraged to choose from the buffet's soups, fruit or vegetable cocktails, entrées, and tempting desserts. The night we dined there, fish, beef stroganoff, and chicken were offered—rather ordinary fare. Service is cafeteria style, with everyone jumping up and down to get different courses. Only coffee is brought to you.

Next time, I would look for the hotel's other, more formal restaurant. It is open only for supper and features evening entertainment—a tradition unique to Guanajuato, where, as in days of old, groups of male students from the University of Guanajuato gather to serenade the public. At Castillo de Santa Cecilia, this tradition is presented in a more formalized stage show.

It took me a while to find the hotel's namesake, up some stairs by the pool to the high, back part of the property. The chapel, which once overlooked a mine shaft, is little more than one small room. Perhaps miners stopped for blessings before descending. The remains of the shaft are now incorporated into the hotel's grounds.

I must say, cleanliness is not the strong point here. Not only were tablecloths spotted at supper, they were still spotted at breakfast. Bedroom carpets showed water damage near the windows, and lint was highly visible. This was partially explained when I saw maids using brooms instead of vacuums. Tile bathroom and hall floors, however, were mopped down.

But what a kick to stay in a glitzy Mexican inn. Just keep looking up, not down.

5

West of Mexico City

I always considered Mexico to be barren mountains and plateaus interspersed with lush, tropical lowlands. So it was with amazement that we first approached Morelia (mor-AY-lee-ah) from Mexico City and found ourselves driving through miles of pine forests. For most of two hours, our little car ascended curve after curve in the quiet forest (often behind slow trucks and buses spewing black smoke) and then descended into the high valley that holds Morelia.

Morelia is a well-preserved colonial city, also capital of its state, where new construction must conform to traditional appearance. The city and its environs present a good example of the Spanish master plan to take over the country. Early Franciscan monks fanned out from Mexico City, converting natives and building cathedrals. Then they fanned out farther, to the smaller villages. They taught or improved techniques in one craft here, a different one there.

That's why market days are so interesting. Most Sundays and Thursdays, natives from different villages set up shop in town, spilling out from the market pavilion into the streets. You can find bright, lacquered inlaid trays; woven wool blankets and rugs; all kinds of baskets; hammocks; *huaraches* (sandals); silver jewelry; copper pieces; pottery; clothing; and, of course, a certain percentage of junk.

If you miss market day, don't worry. You can go to the village where the items on your shopping list are made, and you may even be able to watch artisans at work. Or sign up for a bus tour designed for that purpose. Because of its pleasant, even climate and central location, the area west of Mexico City abounds with attractive places for tourists, so the residents are used to such visits.

Pátzcuaro (PATS-kwair-o), the largest of these towns, is not to be missed even if you left shopping off your agenda. The town is near the long, shallow lake of the same name, and natives bring their specialties to Pátzcuaro's market day, Friday, by boat. Some live on the lake's islands (which tourists may visit); others live along the shore and use the lake as a highway.

Most residents are of Tarascan Indian blood, of slender build, with pointed chins and high cheekbones. They are a proud but friendly group. Pátzcuaro was once their capital, in precolonial times, and it is one of the few Mexican names in which the accent is on the first syllable.

You could explore all of the town center without realizing it is near a lake, for the land is quite flat and the view is limited. Two main plazas are of note. The first, where the market is, bustles with activity every day and is not hard to find. We almost missed the other one, though, and what a pity that would have been. Several blocks from the market plaza and full of fountains, ponds, lawn, benches, and tiled pathways, the four square blocks of this parklike plaza are completely surrounded by preserved colonial buildings and storefronts. Stumbling across it as we did was like going through a time machine. I expected the whole thing to disappear in the blink of an eye. Walking around the square, I saw no soft drink signs, no liquor stores, only open restaurants and stores and official-looking buildings. It is a treasure for students of historical architecture, and well worth a roll of film to show the folks at home.

Villa Montaña

M orelia, near Lake Pátzcaro, has its own jewel of an accommodation in Villa Montaña. Its walled hillside garden with meandering brick paths and stairs connects sixty-five individual quarters in several dozen low structures.

Villa Montaña has a nostalgic place in the hearts of those who discovered it early on, when it was run by Philippe de Reiset. I can imagine the attraction of boarding a flight to Mexico City, flying to Morelia the next morning, and settling into a luxurious room, surrounded by gardens. No menus to choose entrées from, no decisions to make about what to do, and *margaritas* on the house. Very little was offered in the way of distractions, and no activities director intruded on your plans.

Well, the charming host is long gone, to manage a rooming house in Cuernavaca (not Las Mañanitas). Villa Montaña now has a liquor license so the *margaritas* no longer are free. Some people feel that the meals, already paid for, are mediocre at best. Tour buses are now allowed and may suddenly appear, preempting other guests' mealtimes, indeed their very room reservations. Also, unlike most, the staff we encountered were stiff and unfriendly.

One friend, an innkeeper from California, left a note at the office for another innkeeper who was arriving later that month. The second innkeeper didn't receive it until he checked out.

For one who just discovered this place though, most of its attractions still exist. Off a quiet hillside street, the bricked parking lot and paths lead to a windowed bar and sitting area overlooking the flatland where the town is. Flowers and flowering shrubs abound in raised bricked beds, with steps meandering from one level to another. The dining room is appropriately formal and Spanish. It is enjoyed by the public as well as resort guests. A good-sized pool is blocked from breezes on two sides with glassed-in public seating areas. And the unusual central patio is devoted to large stone replicas, principally of fish.

I was shown a suite, number 28, that measured fifty by sixty feet (I paced it off). Its huge two-story-high living room with fireplace has two sofas. The bedroom, up a few steps and almost as large, has its own fireplace, plus two double beds. Off the bedroom is a large tiled bath. Cost was reasonable, considering that it includes all meals for two.

Room 50, a junior suite, is still extravagantly sized. The sitting area has only one sofa, but both it and the raised platform with a king-sized bed share a stupendous view of the town below, with no rooftops intervening. The tiled bath features a sunken tub. This suite costs about $5 less than room 28.

All rooms have fireplaces. Although the weather in Morelia is generally temperate, some winter evenings are cool.

Villa Montaña is a lovely place from which to explore the entire area, and you can easily get here without driving. It is quiet and controlled; no one is liable to intrude on your privacy. A pool and nearby golf and tennis facilities await the energetic. And if you need help, one member of the office staff understands English well.

"If you vacation to catch up on your reading," says the hotel's brochure, or "to write the book you've planned for years," this is the place for you. Villa Montaña offers few activities other than eating, drinking, and lolling by the pool. But each nearby village has its own craft specialty, from baskets to painted trays to woven rugs. Day-long trips to each are easily arranged and can net good buys to take home.

Villa Montaña, Apartado Postal 233, Morelia, Michoagán, Mexico. Telephone (operator assisted) 52-451-2-25-88. 69 rooms and suites. Moderate; meals included.

Mesón del Cortijo

I was apprehensive about our reservations at Mesón del Cortijo. When I called from home, no one was there who spoke English. So I wrote a follow-up letter, hoped it would arrive in time, and crossed my fingers.

Needlessly, it turned out.

The inn is located on the eastern approach to Pátzcuaro, off the noisy highway a few blocks, but nowhere near the architecturally exquisite colonial plaza for which this town is famed.

As we timidly drove into the parking area of the low, red-tile-roofed inn, a lithe man with the sharper features of the natives in this area burst out of the long, similarly constructed building that houses the restaurant. Smiling, he gestured us into a parking spot near the courtyard entry. More gestures and we were in his office identifying ourselves. He drew out my letter asking for reservations, picked three room keys from a board, and ushered us across one of two bougainvillea-drenched brick courtyards to choose a room. At $25, the larger one had a sunken sitting area, full-length windows with wrought-iron grating, two double beds, and a bath on an upper level. The $15 room, which we chose, was almost as large but with less of a view. The view, by the way, is pastoral: a horse grazing on some open land, and a partially completed wing of this inn.

All rooms open onto the courtyard and have red glazed tile floors, white stucco walls, and beamed ceilings with slanted, hand-cut battens. Nicely paneled entry and closet doors and wooden window blinds attested to nearby forests and Indian master craftsmen.

In our room, locally woven throw rugs matched the striped spreads in hot red tones that covered the two beds, a double and a three-quarter. The sitting area had a little stucco fireplace and loveseat. Bottled water in a beautiful blue glass decanter sat on a desk by the door. The bathroom—with its nonslip machine-made tile and walk-in shower—indicated this was not an old structure, as the manager, Rafael Servin, acknowledged. The owner purchased the property twenty years ago. When we were there, the inn had eight completed units; others had been roofed and tiled, but not finished. "Un poquito here, un poquito there," Señor Servin smiled.

Between the two courtyards is a nice sunroom with huge armchairs and a good-sized fireplace.

Nearby, the restaurant is narrow and small but striking and clean. Fuchsia linen curtains enliven French doors and windows. White tablecloths with bright red overcloths and fresh flowers perk up the tables, which seat about sixty. Chamber music quickly replaced the Mexican radio station that was playing when we entered.

Breakfast at the restaurant is $2 extra, but consider this breakfast: lots of freshly squeezed orange juice, a three-egg

Mesón del Cortijo, Apartado Postal 202, Pátzcuaro, Michoagán, Mexico. Telephone (operator assisted) 52-454-2-12-95 or 2-10-37. Rafael Servin, Manager. 12 rooms. Inexpensive.

omelet, sausage, beans, good hot breads with jam, and lots of coffee. Quite a bargain.

The restaurant was closed evenings when we visited in late June. This is off-season for statesiders, but it was not readily evident if the restaurant was not serving because of a seasonal slack or because we were the only ones wishing to dine.

This is the most Mexican of the inns in this book, and perhaps not for everyone. Hot water is available mornings only, and there are no English subtitles on the menu. But everyone who works at Mesón del Cortijo is eager to help you feel at ease, and we got along just fine with a Spanish–English phrase book, a pad, and a pencil.

Posada Don Vasco

_____

S ince the dining room at Mesón del Cortijo was closed for dinner, we walked a few blocks to Posada Don Vasco, a remodeled villa on the lake side of the main road into Pátzcuaro. It seems incongruous, but both this towering old mansion and the squat motel units across the road have the same owners.

Forget the motel units, for that's all they are. The villa's quaint, high-ceilinged rooms have twin beds, modern baths, bottled water, and carpet. The all face a central courtyard with umbrella tables and fire pits. But they are tiny rooms, with just enough room to walk around the beds and no seating area. Instead, guests can use the hotel's sitting room, the size of one of the bedrooms, which contains half a dozen chairs. It would be uncomfortable, though, for more than one party to converse at a time.

All in all, I got the feeling that this hotel had been patched together with the hope that it would somehow work. So unless you can stand the main-street noises and Mexican diesel buses, or you want the security of having someone on the premises who understands English, stay at Mesón del Cortijo.

The restaurant at Posada Don Vasco, on the other hand, is well worth the visit. Its large dining room faces the street downstairs. Yellow and brown checkered tablecloths, fresh flowers on the tables, and big plants soften the stark effect of white stucco walls and fourteen-foot-high beamed ceilings. Service is pleasant, and the menu includes both Mexican and North American favorites. This is a fine place to try the Pátzcuaro specialty, small whitefish.

Our excellent dinner with _tortilla_ soup cost very little and included nonstop entertainment by an accomplished singer/guitarist, all in Spanish. Entertainment is one reason the restaurant is favored by North Americans, and at least half the people filling the room that night were fellow tourists.

On Wednesday evenings, the hotel presents a group of masked dancers performing *los viejitos*, the "dance of the little old men." Young boys armed with canes portray the shakes and weaknesses of old age as well as the ever-present love of life. There is no charge for this performance, a local tradition.

Pátzcuaro is far enough off the beaten track between Mexico City and Guadalajara to be skipped over by those who have not heard of its beautiful lake and the architecture of its Spanish colonial plaza (see the introduction to this chapter). We happened to hit the town's market day and brought home great buys in lacquered trays, baskets, woven Christmas tree decorations, and woven rugs—not all those bright hot colors favored in most of Mexico, but subdued themes.

Your Spanish–English dictionary will come in handy, for few residents understand English. I spent an uneasy hour trying to find a common digestive aid in one of two pharmacies on

Posada Don Vasco, Calzada de las Americas, Apartado 15, Concido, Pátzcuaro, Michoagán, Mexico. Telephone (operator assisted) 52-454-2-02-27 or 2-02-62. 100 rooms. Inexpensive.

the plaza and finally resorted to pointing, pad, and pencil.

This is also the town where we found ourselves driving the wrong way on a one-way street. The *policía* found us also. After ten minutes of trying to understand each other, we turned to the "common phrases" section of the phrase book and found something that meant "Please excuse us, we did not mean to do wrong." It worked.

6

Guadalajara & Lake Chapala

I f you were inclined to become familiar with a large Mexican city, would you choose the largest—noisy, smoggy, and full of traffic and homeless beggars—or the second largest—clean, graced by wide boulevards, a recently renovated downtown area with plenty of parks, friendly people, new shopping centers, and well-kept colonial structures?

Guadalajara has all these advantages and more. Its principal cathedral, instead of facing a main square, is surrounded by four plazas. Four is an important number here, for the city is separated into four sections, each with its own names for streets. Getting lost in Guadalajara is easy.

The area has constant springlike weather. Even in the rainy season, June through September, showers are confined to afternoon or evening spurts. Such amenities have attracted an English-speaking populace large enough to support a weekly newspaper, which tourists can purchase to see what special events are scheduled. These are often worth knowing about, since Guadalajara is normally light on nightlife. Fiesta dances, for example, are often held in the cultural center, a magnificent nineteenth-century building filled with gold leaf and ornamental crystal. Tickets are only a few pesos.

Guadalajara's surroundings are also of note. Right on the city's border is Tlaquepaque (tlah-kay-PAH-kay), a fine native crafts center about a dozen blocks square. This is a treasure trove of hand-painted china and pottery, rattan, stoneware, sculpture, blown glass, carved wood, onyx chess sets, woven garments, heavy rugs, and other fine crafts. Merchants here sell out of stores rather than village markets. Almost all shopkeepers know English, accept credit cards, and will even arrange to ship purchases.

An intriguing place for lunch in Tlaquepaque is the Restaurant with No Name (no connection to the one in San Francisco, points out its owner). Exotic birds roam the inner courtyard while diners sample quiche, fruits, and the best alcoholic soda I've ever tasted, a kahlua concoction. No sign hangs out front, but don't worry about finding it: It's marked on an English-language walking guide and map handed out at the shops.

About thirty-five miles south of Guadalajara is Lake Chapala, largest in Mexico. It's a bit shallow now, but still sixty-five miles long and a third as wide. This is a favorite weekend getaway for Guadalajara businesspeople. A pier lined with gambling casinos once ran from the bottom of Chapala's main street into the lake, but one of the country's leaders who opposed gambling had it burned.

Chapala is rather a busy town, with grocery and drug stores, banks, and travel agents. Most North American and European residents are retirees, many from the military, as is the case in the nearby villages of Ajijic (ah-hee-HEEK) and Chula Vista. Lately, successful entrepreneurs from those countries are joining the older group and restoring antique homes for modern use. Mexican residents still outnumber foreigners in these towns, with the exception of Chula Vista.

Ajijic, one of several quaint villages around the lake, is known for its fine weavers. Soft woolen dresses and sweaters are sold in several factory/shops. Farther west along the lake is Jocotepec, where weavers specialize in white *serapes*.

One could easily adjust to the low-keyed life around Guadalajara and Lake Chapala. It's tempting, until one chats with *gringo* residents who congregate daily at Posada Ajijic, hungry for news for the States and complaining about unreliable labor and the dollar crunch.

Quinta Quetzalcóatl

M ost similar to American bed and breakfast inns is Quinta Quetzalcóatl (KEEN-tah ket-zal-CO-ah-tul), or "Inn of the Plumed Serpent." The winged serpent is a god from Aztec/Toltec mythology. Near the shores of Lake Chapala, this establishment is run by a California couple for the unsullied pleasure of their guests. Barbi Henderson and her husband, Dick, meet you at the Guadalajara airport, provide huge breakfasts and suppers, host day-long tours of surrounding villages and craft centers, and even have a courtesy bar. You need never struggle to communicate across a language barrier with taxi drivers and others.

This is not to say that the Hendersons protect you from the least inkling that you are in a foreign country. Barbi brings Mexican culture, food, decorations, and language into every aspect of the inn. (Dick, who also runs a nautical-goods store in California, was not at the inn during our visit, so my impressions are of his wife.)

The oldest part of the house is where *The Plumed Serpent* was written by a besotted D. H. Lawrence (whose later book, *Lady Chatterley's Lover*, was banned in Boston). When the Hendersons bought the house about five years ago, they found a large painting of the author. Barbi's brown eyes must have lit up when she thought of Lawrence's penchant for strong, lusty heroines. What a place for a romantic inn!

Barbi possesses a number of the same qualities as a Lawrence character. Well endowed physically and talented in many areas, she has a spark that invigorates the inn. Her vivid imagination and graphic arts training in San Miguel de Allende help her envision the inn's future rooms. Meanwhile, shopping "finds" become key elements in existing rooms. Where else would you open the doors of a floor-to-ceiling armoire to discover a bathroom? A mirrored Mexican tile sink is behind one door, and the walk-in skylit shower and water closet are behind the other.

This particular whimsy is in the second-story quarters known as Lady Chatterley's Room. She is personified by the delicate marble bust of a woman with a Mona Lisa smile, her unapproachable grandeur somewhat offset by the locket and pale pink beribboned hat the hostess has added. Ruffles and lace abound in pale pink, blue, and white. You can't even rest on the king-sized bed until you remove a dozen frilly pillows. A spindly French provincial writing desk, white with a pink wash, echoes the finish of other main pieces in the room. Although Lawrence's books occupy the desktop, he would probably feel

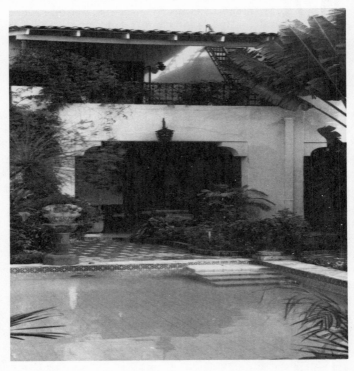

Quinta Quetzalcóatl, Señor Ricardo Henderson y Señora, Apartado Postal 286, Caragoza No. 307, 45900 Chapala, Jalisco, Mexico. Telephone (operator assisted) 91-376-5-36-53. *Also for reservations*: P.O. Box 27, Point Richmond, CA 94807. Telephone (415) 562-5145. Dick and Barbi Henderson, hosts and owners. 9 rooms. Minimum stay: 1 week. Expensive; meals and many extras included.

uncomfortable sitting on the fragile chair. The French touches fit in culturally, though, for France ruled Mexico for a time.

Where are the signs of Lady Chatterley's secret lover, the gamekeeper? In a boxy woven rattan armoire, next to a lady's pink satin bathrobe, is a blue-striped seersucker robe. And for today's practical male guest, a native pottery tray holds instant coffee makings for early risers. How many guests, one wonders, have slipped on the robes for a few hours of make-believe?

One can spend days sitting by the small, shallow pool here. But it's hard not to follow Barbi as she zings out of her room, across the courtyard, on her way to "the most marvelous restaurant" in, say, Tlaquepaque, a nearby artisan's center. The Hendersons have a fifteen-seat van and limit the number of guests accordingly, though the inn has quarters for nearly twenty around the courtyard.

Suppers follow the do-it-yourself cocktail hour and tend to be good, huge, and showy—on the order of bringing in a perfectly cooked pork roast by the light of festive sparklers. And four freshly cooked vegetables at one meal may be a bit much, but never boring.

Festival night dinner, the evening of arrival, brings on a guitar-playing trio, with the hostess emitting regular Mexican yips of encouragement here and there. Dressed in white, she joins the singers in a special song about Lake Chapala and love.

Breakfast, served on a round, hide-covered table by the pool, might consist of canteloupe heaped with cinnamon-topped yogurt, individual baking dishes of *guacamole* topped with egg and cheese, hot baked breads, bacon, and Mexican hot chocolate. Barbi, chef for this breakfast, told us how hard it is to train help: part of the meal was late because her helper, when told to fry the bacon, got out lard to fry it in. The staff of four, who have been with the inn for some time, actually know quite a bit of basic English. But as Barbi's running patter demonstrated, misunderstood directions and odd results can be hilarious in the telling.

From mailings to guests when they reserve space, to little sheets of information in the rooms, everything at Quinta Quetzalcóatl is in plain English, and you always know what to expect. Visits here are by the week only, so you may eventually want some time to yourself. Barbi will supply all you need to know for a day on your own. You can taxi to golf or tennis facilities, go shopping, visit the local hot springs, or enjoy the night life. And you can always return to the feeling of togetherness that permeates this utterly unique inn.

Posada Ajijic

A few miles from Chapala, Posada Ajijic's walled complex presents a different experience for the traveler. Ajijic (ah-hee-HEEK), though small in population, has a high concentration of English-speaking residents: 2,500 at last count. These expatriates' informal meeting place is the bar of Posada Ajijic, where the vacationer hungry for the sound of English will find instant friends anxious to tell about the area. Beware the *margaritas*, though, for they are big, excellent, inexpensive, and *strong*.

As with many Mexican inns, this one includes an award-winning restaurant, a dance floor, and live music in the evening. Mexican families also frequent the restaurant, which overlooks the lake and has immense style, as attested by its framed letters from *Gourmet* and *Bon Appetit* magazines. Indeed, it is the perfect place to try the famed local delicacy, whitefish. Also recommended is the *ceviche* (raw fish cocktail) and the curried shrimp served in generous portions with East Indian–style condiments. The host, Mike Eager, caters to Canadian and U.S. palates as well as offering selected Mexican specialties.

Mike's Canadian parents bought Posada Ajijic sight unseen in 1975. Parts of it are 300 years old; it once was the *hacienda* of the area's Spanish landlords, who also had a corn mill here. Then, after a stint as a private home, the building became a center for making ingots from gold mined in nearby hills. Mike says the garden is built on tailings.

Next came a *tequila* factory, and the bathroom of suite 14 served as the distillery. Later, *tortillas* were manufactured here. Then Josefina Ramirez purchased it. She had a great deal to do with promoting and organizing the local hand-loomed wool industry. During World War II, she let foreign visitors build their own cottages in corners of the block-square walled compound.

Her husband grew coffee plants and sold his crops to Germany. After the war, two Englishmen purchased the *posada* for hotel use. It subsequently became a health spa, at which ladies of the night were also available.

The owners who preceded the senior Eagers had gone bankrupt. When the Canadian couple came to claim possession, they found the place stripped of electric cords, bathroom tiles, fixtures—everything. It took them six months to restore. Now the main *hacienda* houses the kitchen, dining room, bar, and small dance floor. Outbuildings of various ages serve as lobby, office, supply storehouse, and fourteen guest quarters, hidden away in different corners of the garden. The prize accommodation, given its central location plus historical novelty, is the *tequila* distillery suite.

We stayed in 12A, a suite with white wicker in the sitting

Posada Ajijic, Apartado Postal 30, Ajijic, Jalisco, Mexico. Telephone (operator assisted) 52-376-5-33-95. Mike and Maria Eager, hosts. 14 rooms and suites. Inexpensive.

room, a comfortable king-sized bed in the large bedroom, and a large, tiled bathroom. The carved wooden furnishings and ceiling beams are simple but suitable, as are the locally woven matching bedspread and curtains. A small fireplace indicates that heat is needed only a half dozen times a year. Two types of tile in the bath show that the Eagers did some restoration here. Hot water? Yes, but it takes forever unless you use the shower faucet.

A large pool beckons in the garden, and a poolside bar supplies soup and sandwiches. In his office to the rear, Mike maintains a lending library of paperbacks. When we visited, he was also planning a small restaurant in the pool area specifically to prepare and serve *carnitas brasas*, thinly sliced beef and pork tenderloin in its own juices.

Meanwhile, the price of a room for two is around $20, and meals are comparatively inexpensive. The main restaurant and bar, in the oldest part of the complex, look right onto Lake Chapala, the beach where locals ride by on burros, and the town's dock, which stretches far into the shallow lake. It's easy to envy those who have made this temperate spot their permanent home.

Hotel Real de Chapala

———————

Part way between Chapala and Ajijic, a nice eighty-room resort hotel stretches along two acres of lakefront under a eucalyptus grove. The approach is dramatic: Flame trees line several blocks of wide boulevards. Rough cobblestones pave the way, and grass grows between them like green velvet. You pass the entrance to the local yacht club but no other buildings, just lawns and paths under the old trees. Perhaps you'll glimpse a few hotel guests on horseback, or residents aboard overloaded mules.

Long before famous people discovered Chapala, this property was an orchard. The weather here was—and is—ideal, even more so than in Chapala. At a temperate 5,200-foot altitude, it is protected by hills and cooled by breezes from the lake.

Hotel Real de Chapala, fourteen years old, is now owned by the nearby university. Jacaranda trees and bougainvillea vines flower along the open walkways between wings of this rambling two-story Mexican-style building. Underfoot, lizards zip along keeping down the insect population.

The hotel features several restaurants as well as a cafeteria. It has two pools, tennis courts, a volleyball court, ping-pong tables, and a game room. In deference to vacationing families, babysitting is offered as well.

Rooms are in a long two-story wing with doors off a central hall. Huge and high-ceilinged, they are more like suites: the suggestion of an archway separates a sitting area from the bedroom, which is furnished in heavy, dark wood dressers and headboards for the two double beds. Each room has a patio or porch; half face the lake, half the landscaped grounds.

The hotel often presents weekend dinner shows featuring local entertainment. We happened to arrive on July 4 when, in honor of the area's many stateside residents, the hotel had prepared a special show. On the restaurant's central stage, young singers and dancers performed favorites from the States, in Spanish, while waitresses brought course after course to our table. Between the two of us, we sampled cactus salad, whitefish hors d'oeuvres, green bean soup, *tortilla* soup, beefsteak (quite tender, for once), a soft, chicken-filled *tortilla*, hot *guacamole*, a small chicken tart, beans, and caramel custard, or *flan*, a favorite Mexican dessert. In honor of the occasion, coconut candies wrapped in red, white, and green—Mexico's colors—were presented as well.

The next evening, we attended an outdoor buffet on the patio by the lake, where we chose from an equally broad range of local food specialties. The hotel caters principally to vacationing Mexican families; we were able to do quite well with our Spanish–English dictionary and a lot of smiling.

While staying here, you might want to drive west along the lake to Jocotepec, a small town where hand-loomed garments are made. Partway, at San Juan Cosalá, a series of cement pools capture naturally heated water from fissures in the earth. We stopped, changed in the dressing rooms, and soaked in a smaller pool whose water was 112 degrees Fahrenheit, then plunged into cooler waters. There's a snack bar there, but no suits or towels to rent, so bring your own.

Hotel Real de Chapala, Apartado Postal 333, Ajijic, Jalisco, Mexico. Telephone (operator assisted) 52-732-5-24-16. 80 rooms; five suites with small swim pools. Inexpensive.

7

Alamos

Alamos has an uncommon hold on certain people. It is "a place that speaks to one in a certain way," says innkeeper Darley Fuller Gordon, owner of Casa de los Tesoros. "It takes over the person, not the other way around. Newcomers are smitten the same way I was thirty-one years ago, even though the town is entirely different now."

I can attest to the attraction.

Alamos, whose name means "cottonwood," is an hour's drive from the main coastal road that connects the state of Sonora with Arizona and Texas. Perched in the foothills, it surveys the flatlands between the Gulf of California and the Sierra Madre, an area rich with agriculture. To the south, at a protected port near Los Mochis, imports arrive while produce embarks for the rest of the country.

A silver town, Alamos was farthest from Cortés' clutches but was tapped by those who followed. Still, a lot of silver money stayed at home and made Alamos what it is today. And a goodly portion funded Father Junipero Serra's 1769 trek up Baja California to San Diego and beyond. Many of his entourage were Alamos residents, who helped establish the missions that still dot California.

I had no business in Sonora other than checking out Alamos inns, so my approach was by air, over the Sea of Cortez to Los Mochis, then inland by rental car. The road, for the most part, was fast and straight; and the approach to the hilly town was normal enough: pass a plaza, bear to the right, and drive a few blocks.

But then something happens. All around, for eight or ten square blocks, are beautifully restored homes in the Andalusian style of architecture, from Seville and Cadiz, Spain. Quiet streets are smoothly paved with interlocking cobblestones. A central cathedral faces a neat plaza and delicately fluted, iron-edged gazebo. An appropriate mural covers the gazebo's ceiling. Everything is in order, painted, and in repair. And it is so quiet that the sound of a closing door echoes. Few people are in evidence, for it is late June and the owners of these homes are back in the United States until fall.

It's like driving around an outdoor museum. In fact, the town of Alamos is a national colonial monument. Exterior architecture must remain unaltered in appearance.

Darley Gordon, who has taken part in Alamos' recent revival, told me more of this unique place from her summer quarters near San Francisco. In the early 1700s, when a number of its mines were producing silver and iron, Alamos became a thriving city. But measles, smallpox, and famine took 6,000 lives in 1750, causing the surveyor general to recommend wealthy citizens rebuild their houses with adjoining walls. This would eliminate cubbyholes that sheltered the poor—then believed to have caused the plague.

In the ensuing half century, the well-off built their homes near the cathedral, first for protection against Indian attacks, then for status. The whole preserved area is thus approximately the same age and architecture. The Spanish influence of the surveyor general is most visible in the bulbous Doric columns supporting arch after arch, in arcades in front of large homes, and in the iron filigree that covers windows and gates.

Silver flowed from mines at Alamos throughout revolts and unrest but decreased to a trickle by the turn of this century. The town was deserted by 1930, left to prospectors with pickaxes looking for the buried metal. Then, in the early 1950s, people from the United States rediscovered Alamos as a place to reside in comfort and style at very low cost. Today, more than 150 American families live there.

Alamos natives are proud of their heritage and their contribution to the town as it exists today. Local labor helped build and now staffs these homes, creating a profitable interdependence with the new residents.

Casa de los Tesoros

———

Darley Fuller Gordon has owned and run the venerable Casa de los Tesoros ("house of riches" or "treasure house") for more than thirty years. Early in the 1950s, she and her then husband, both writers and educational filmmakers who found Alamos close enough to Hollywood and film assignments, were among the first wave of new settlers. Another writer, Enrique Rios, and his wife, Mariena, joined them from San Miguel de Allende, where they'd owned a small inn (see Villa Santa Monica). In Alamos, they opened Casa de los Tesoros. Erected in 1789 for the padre Juan Nicholas y Mora, the building had later become a convent where nuns taught children.

Enrique Rios subsequently became ill, and he and his family moved away. By then, though, the government had declared Alamos a historic preserve. Since no other hostelry existed, and since most of the town's new homeowners stayed at the inn before purchasing property, officials wanted Casa de los Tesoros to remain an inn. And that's how Darley came into the hotel business.

Like most of the town's structures, the inn is rectangular and has a covered inner arcade and patio. Doors to each room are off this arcade, which protects them from rain and sun alike. At each door, a little tin "house" holds a candle for use in case of power failure.

A small chapel, now a dining room, separates the front and back patios. Its confessional is now a bar. Masses of vines, which burst into orange blossoms January through March, hang over a more informal arcade to the rear, by a five-foot-deep swimming pool. This back area housed horses and other animals.

Slender columns support the front arcade. Here and there, informal conversational groupings of hide-covered or wrought iron furnishings serve as sitting areas for the fourteen guest rooms. To the front of the house is an indoor living room with a desk, writing supplies, a few games, and books. A little gift shop features clothing and hats; artwork by Roberto Bloor, a young Canadian artist and Darley's partner; and a few small pamphlets Darley has written about Alamos.

Our room, which inn manager Edith de Pratt called "the best one," was to the very back, where the carriage and horses were originally kept. Heavy black iron bolts open the ancient, narrow wooden double doors through walls three feet thick. You step down onto big woven rugs covering the rough, dark tile floor. More woven spreads and loosely woven cotton sheets cover the double bed and the daybed in the corner. A little sitting area with a hard church-pew bench and a coffee table adjoins the small fireplace. Desk and dresser complete the room's furnishings.

It's hard to comprehend fireplaces in this tropical location, but Edith says they are needed some winter nights. Meanwhile, it was June, so we were glad to see the iced purified water placed in the room by one of several white-coated men, all of

Casa de los Tesoros, Calle Obregon 10, Apartado Postal 12, Alamos, Sonora, Mexico. Telephone (operator assisted) 52-642-8-00-10. Edith de Pratt, manager; Darley Fuller Gordon and Roberto Bloor, owners. 14 rooms, most with private baths. Some freestanding fans. Inexpensive; includes meals in season. Check to see if open May–October.

whom proved most friendly, obliging, and knowledgeable in basic English.

After settling in, we headed for the restaurant. Darley's co-owner, Roberto, has excelled in training the kitchen staff and refining the menus, and our first taste of his talents proved to be the best *margarita* of the trip. In a country filled with limes, most restaurants have retreated to commercial *margarita* mixes and blenders, but this was fresh. Its small pellets of ice didn't instantly turn to slush and thin the concoction, and the drink was accompanied by the best *nacho* chips I've had on either side of the border.

Our dinner, after delicate meatball soup, was a Sonora ranch type, with braised beef, *taco* with meat and lettuce, and lots of cheese. During the summer, when fewer North Americans visit, the fare is simpler and served à la carte. Winter menus might include Waldorf salad, bean and chocolate soup, seafood crêpes, stuffed monkey shirts (Mexican pastry filled with ground beef and vegetables, deep-fried, and then baked), and mint teacakes. In season, there's also Saturday night Mayo dancing in the courtyard.

Breakfast was icy cold grapefruit juice and a lightly browned omelet with onion, ham, and cheese, still bubbling hot.

Next time I would go in season, which is October through April. I don't like the bugs and humidity that characterize the rainy summer months. But I would definitely go again. As Darley says, "Alamos is not a place, it's a feeling"—a unique feeling I would like to repeat.

8

The Mexican Riviera

From Puerto Vallarta to Acapulco, a handful of blissful sun-and-fun vacation destinations appear most frequently in large Sunday paper travel sections: Yelapa, Manzanillo, Ixtapa, Zihuatanejo, and the two anchor cities. What the ads don't mention is that the package price for two usually includes a room or condo twelve flights up in a highrise on a bluff. You and hundreds of others end up around the hotel pool because the ocean is either too rough for swimming right there, or too far away.

It is possible, though, to lie in the tropical sun on a clean, sandy beach and enjoy the ambience of a romantic Mexican inn. These oceanside inns, all built in this century, make up in uniqueness what they miss in centuries-old history. And although they all share the same ocean, each town is distinctly different. On a thin strip of land between waves and mountains, Puerto Vallarta is a fishing village with cobblestone streets. Purists claim it has been spoiled by all the resorts along the highway south of the town's center, but most of this growth is out of sight. Strolling the streets downtown captures the sights, sounds, and flavors of Mexico. Off the beaten path, natives still wash their clothes in the river that bisects the town.

The truly small village of Yelapa makes no such claims. On a peninsula south of Puerto Vallarta, it is accessible only by a two-hour boat ride, once a day. In fact, the day's big excitement is when that boat arrives. All the residents get out their merchandise and head for the beach. To enjoy Yelapa fully, tourists stay overnight at one of the village's two establishments.

Manzanillo is half a day's drive south from Puerto Vallarta on a narrow road that threads its way around mountain shoulders and ravines. Finally the land flattens and you descend into a sea of coconut palms and banana plantations, more than I've seen in a lifetime in California. The city is not a major resort town, but rather a shipping port of great importance to Mexico. Its docks are loaded with manufactured goods and produce destined for other countries. Even so, the protected harbor has beautiful beaches and a constant temperature of 80 degrees.

Ixtapa (ees-TAH-pah) is another Cancún, a mile-long stretch of beach lined by tall hotels with familiar chain names. Some Mexican tourist study determined this to be the perfect location for such a concentration, but the strong undertow precludes swimming.

For a perfect contrast, visit Zihuatanejo, (zee-wah-tah-NAY-ho), a fishing village five miles away. While benefiting from its new neighbor and visitors, it retains its character. More gift shops and restaurants line the bumpy streets than before, but neon has not yet arrived. On a protected bay, swimming is only a few steps from Zihuatanejo's inns.

Acapulco, southernmost of these towns, is a favorite of both Mexicans and foreigners. Cruise ships and many airlines land here, and a good road stretches to Mexico City. Air-conditioning is necessary to ensure comfort this far south, and the tall hotels lining the white beaches must have it to survive. If soaking in sun on the beach is your principal desire, shop around for a travel package and pack up. But be prepared for an unbelievable number of persistent sidewalk and beach vendors who trail you to the ocean's very edge as you wade in. Prices are usually higher here than inland or at other resorts, for wily merchants know that many tourists make this their only Mexican stop.

Cortés made it all the way to this western coast, so historic sites are near most vacation destinations. Ask the innkeeper. And meanwhile, enjoy the romance of tropical breezes, sunsets on the Pacific, and dining on lobster in the company of someone special.

Hotel Posada Rio Cuale

O ver dinner at the Hotel Posada Rio Cuale, we watched as a party of six from Texas settled in. When asked if they would like cocktails before dinner, one gentleman said of his companion, "She'll have the largest banana daiquiri you have."

We sat back, grinned, and waited. Sure enough, when the heavy glass goblet arrived, holding a good sixteen ounces, all the lady could say was, "Holy Moses, forget the menu."

The twenty-year-old Hotel Posada Rio Cuale, where the river meets the sea, is right downtown where all the action is. A few blocks north, John Huston paid to have a bridge built so he could film it in *Night of the Iguana*. But Mexicans own and run this hotel and, to date, Americans know of it only because of its accomplished kitchen and staff. For example, the Texans were staying at Garza Blanca, the expensive digs south of town. Nevertheless, the manager and almost everyone else in direct contact with guests at Hotel Posada Rio Cuale know basic English, so language problems seldom arise.

Around the dining patio and terrace, a loose collection of white stucco and rough brick structures contain guests' quarters. Hand-painted flowers decorate the doors and the white bathroom walls, where patterned blue tile lines the stall showers. The bedroom floors feature dark blue slate tiles. Varnished vertical lath adorns some walls; varnished brick, others. Most rooms have double beds; bright blue spreads covered candy-striped sheets on our twin beds. The bedroom also held a desk/dressing table and chair, a small closet with a latticework door, and a raffia bench for bags. The sitting area for our little room, the hotel's last vacancy, was a bench outside on a tiny patio.

The rooms' slatted windows are now glassed in and air-conditioning has superceded the ceiling fan, although it is still there if you prefer. And for once, the light is enough to read by, if per chance you don't spend all your time out promenading the little town's streets or dropping into hole-in-the-wall night spots for some musical entertainment.

A better room is number 208. It's larger, farther from main-street traffic, tucked away to the rear by the pool. And upstairs are other larger rooms—218 through 221—with two double beds and a sitting area large enough for a sofa.

We arrived midafternoon and headed straight for the pool, planning to spend the rest of the day exploring Puerto Vallarta. But after one of those giant *margaritas*, we just relaxed in chaise lounges, listened to the clanging cathedral bells, and watched pedestrians outside the gate until the pool closed at 7 P.M. and dinner guests began arriving.

Hotel Posada Rio Cuale, Aquiles Serdan 242 E Ignacio L. Vallarta, Apartado Postal 146, Puerto Vallarta, Jalisco, Mexico 48300. Telephone (operator assisted) 2-04-50. Jose Luis Hernandez, general manager. 21 rooms and suites. Inexpensive; prices include taxes. Air-conditioning and overhead fans.

Plants are all over the open bar and restaurant. The bartender works out of a thatch-roofed gazebo. Some of the tables are on the tiled patio; others are under a bamboo-roofed courtyard. Life-sized parrots are painted on the walls. In one corner, a piano draped with red cloth came into use early that evening. Two alternating pianists turned out rippling Hoagy Carmichael selections, with barely a pause between players.

Overhead fans with enameled light globes help keep the lights low and the mood intimate. Lacy table covers and fresh flowers heighten the effect. Iced water and butter balls suspended over ice were set before us first by a fast-footed waiter. The waiters here help each other serve large orders quickly, signaling for aid with kissing noises.

Adding to the romance of this restaurant are the many dishes, both entrées and desserts, flamed at the table. We ordered soup, then orange and Cointreau-flavored fresh shrimp. After turning off the ceiling fan to keep from blowing out the flame, the waiter flashed knives and peeled the orange in one perfect long strip. Next came the flame, splashes of this and that in the pan, and, finally, many delectable shrimp. Diners at surrounding tables watched the show. Our delicious dish barely served, the waiter wheeled in another set of props to flame a fancy dessert at a nearby table.

One can afford to spend some time patronizing this restaurant and hotel. Our dinner for two was under $20, and the room was less than $35. Prices rise 20 percent in season, but that's still a bargain.

Nuevo Hotel Lagunita Yelapa

A nd now, a tropical spot for incurable romantics who want to get far, far away from it all—and don't mind roughing it a bit. The power might fail, you could run out of ice cubes, and you can't call home, but...

Getting to Nuevo Hotel Lagunita Yelapa (Yah-LAH-pah) is half the fun. It is inaccessible by road, so your adventure starts at the Puerto Vallarta dock. You board a boat filled with tourists out for a day of swimming, snorkeling, and dining at this sparsely populated tropical cove.

The two-hour ride takes you south along Mexico's lush western coast. Passengers used to splash through waves the last few yards to shore. Now, the boat ties up and unloads at the new dock. You climb from the boat's deck up old tires attached to the side of the pier.

The approach couldn't be more picturesque. Palms and dense tropical foliage cover everything in sight but the white sandy beach. Few structures are in sight, and most of those have thatched roofs. The hotel is actually a series of one-room thatched *palapas*, or huts, and an open-sided restaurant near the beach's north edge.

The boat, chock full of tourists, is like a magnet to every self-employed entrepreneur in the region. They descend on you unmercifully, for they know the tourists will be gone in a few hours and they'll have to wait until the next day to make another sale. Don't worry. When the boat sounds its whistle, the day-trippers climb aboard and all but a sprinkling of beach vendors melt into the jungle. The enchanted beach is yours again until the boat returns around noon the next day.

Other people charter a boat to get to Yelapa, and some

arrive without reservations. There is at least one accommodation other than Hotel Lagunita Yelapa—a cottage run by Miki Shapiro (Apartado Postal 325, Puerto Vallarta).

Not much is on the beach but some *palapas* to protect swimmers from the sun and a few open restaurants, in which the chefs cook over small fires. These cater mostly to the daytime tourists.

Water from a river seeps into the ocean, making periodic gulleys in the smooth sand. Nearby, snorkeling and scuba diving gear, boats for fishing, and horses to ride are for rent on the beach.

But first, check in at the hotel's small office building (open 10 A.M. to 5 P.M.), take your bags to your assigned *palapa*, and settle in. On first impression, the hut seems rather primitive: cement floor, simple construction, and no glass windows (openings are screened and shuttered). But everything you need in a tropical paradise is present: a double bed, dresser, a couple of chairs, a full bathroom with shower (no tub), bottled water, and sun, sun, sun. The view is of the cove, and out the front door is a little patio on which you can sit and enjoy it. The huts are scattered in the tropical growth on different levels, so you're not eyeballing guests on either side.

You may on occasion be eyeing the local fauna, though.

Nuevo Hotel Lagunita Yelapa, Apartado Postal 268, Puerto Vallarta, Jalisco, Mexico. No phone. 23 *palapas,* or huts. Moderate; no meals included. No air-conditioning or fans.

Iguanas are everywhere. One guest was somewhat more than startled the first morning to find one in the bathroom, very big and very green. Mosquitos are also bothersome at times, so you can drop a net down over the double bed, just as at children's camps in the eastern United States.

And if you go down to the bar before the dinner hour (the bar opens at 10 A.M.), you may see your dinner fish being brought in by boat. Can't get much fresher. Accordingly, the regular menu for all meals is heavy on locally caught fish and seafood, which is superb. It also includes something for the meat-and-potatoes type, which is passable. But the pies! Homemade lemon meringue and banana are delicious—and perfectly safe to eat.

A short postprandial stroll provides a glimpse of Yelapa's modest attractions. An artist and her husband run the village's one shop, which sells some interesting things. You can walk or ride horses or ponies to the waterfall; on the way, you'll pass the *tortilla* factory where residents stand in line to get theirs fresh. By the rocks in the bay, exotic fish are close in and visible to snorkelers except when the water is turbulent.

At 10 P.M. the lights go out and you're on your own with a flashlight. Yelapa relies totally on propane gas to generate electricity, and lights after ten are not top priority. Then again, one doesn't travel to the isolated coast of a tropical paradise to stay up all night playing cards.

La Posada

O nce you fly in to Manzanillo, you might as well stay and unwind. Driving the coastal highway in this area means negotiating narrow, curving roads across washed out sections and up and down mountains. It isn't worth it. Fly in and out.

Manzanillo is not a major resort town, but rather a shipping port for produce and manufactured goods. Trucks loaded with goods converge on its protected harbor and enclosed yacht basin. Nonetheless, tourists will find sandy white beaches, marvelous lobster, and an 80-degree temperature year round. Though there is a high and low season as far as accommodation rates go.

Southern Californian Bart Varelmann acquired the shambles of a building here "practically free" after a 1959 hurricane slammed waves over the midsection of Manzanillo's bay. He rebuilt it into La Posada, which now sprawls along the edge of a very nice swimming beach. Just a low seawall separates its patios and twenty-three rooms from the surf. No taking the elevator up six flights and turning left to find your room here. And gazing south about five miles, to the inside of the bay's protective southern arm, you can see downtown Manzanillo and its dock areas.

At the heart of this inn is an open room the size of a small barn. Windowed barn-type doors, seldom closed, are all that separate it from the pool area. Colorful woven spreads cover daybeds randomly placed around the tiled floors, along with tables for games and cards, three comfortable cats, a huge cribbage board, a chess set, and books left by other guests. Framed watercolors and artwork hang here and there.

In one corner, a wooden flowercart on bicycle wheels and with a red fringe on top has been painted passionate pink and converted to bar use. When Bart is not at home, a friendly English-speaking manager takes your order, which is eventually added to your bill. Or you can take a soft drink or beer from the refrigerator by the kitchen. To keep track, drop the cap or ring into the little terra cotta bowl bearing your room number; the caps will be added up when you check out. This bowl is also where you leave your two-inch black iron key when stepping out on the town.

Are you getting the idea that this place is informal? You're right.

The whole *hacienda* is the same passionate pink as the flower-cart. So are the rings painted around the many palm trees. But the paint was chipped here and there when we visited, and the small hourglass-shaped pool needed more frequent cleaning.

Our room was one of the closest to the ocean. It had a slight mildew odor and contained the familiar hide-covered chairs and table; two beds—one a double, thank goodness; and a heavy dresser. Windows front and back were screened and covered with adjustable louvers, so we could hear the waves all night. Our primitive key didn't lock the Dutch door securely, so we said a little prayer and turned off the light. But nothing in the room was valuable enough to make off with, except a raffia-wrapped bottle for purified water that might look quaint at home. But then it would have to be replaced, and that might take months.

The bath and shower were through an open arch and behind a partial brick wall. I'll readily admit it isn't romantic to listen to your partner brush teeth. And since when is a toilet paper holder considered a frill? Nevertheless, you *can* step outside, listen to the ocean roar, and forget a lot.

Storms had made the ocean surf too rough for me, so I went swimming in the hotel's shallow figure-eight pool after dinner. A raincloud drifted over and dumped its contents, but I just swam under a little footbridge that crosses the narrow middle of the pools and waited it out. Later, sitting under a palm tree, it felt wonderful to be in solitary communication with the vast Pacific Ocean, watching the lights of Manzanillo on the other arm of the crescent-shaped bay.

Breakfast from the open kitchen is juice and your choice of *huevos rancheros*, cheese omelet, hotcakes, bacon, and beverages—a large meal considering the price of the room. No supper is served, but lunch consists of sandwiches or soup. I would choose soup; the kitchen is open-sided.

Several of Manzanillo's restaurants were recommended, and we had the best lobster of our trip at Restaurant Bugatti. Sea-food isn't as inexpensive as in earlier years, for it is now trucked inland to a central government warehouse and thence to restaurants, instead of going direct from fishing boat to restaurant. In the interlude, something happens to the price—and sometimes the quality as well.

For what Bart calls "the best *langostinos* lobster you'll ever eat," and the chance to see a local natural phenomenon—a giant green wave that swells up out of nowhere—you might want to rent a car for the day and drive south to Pascuales. Or do as a fellow visitor from Texas did. She was in the process of opening an inn south of Dallas when all the necessary details went awry. She grabbed a bag of books and beach coverups, booked her flight, and stayed put at La Posada for a few days of quiet.

My partner and photographer did not appreciate the rustic charm of La Posada. On the other hand, I am willing to do without a lot of amenities to have contact with the salt spray and soothing presence of the ocean.

La Posada, Podo 135, Manzanillo, Colima, Mexico. Telephone (operator assisted) 22-404 or (800) 252-0211. Bart Varelman, owner/host. 23 units, all next to ocean. Inexpensive; breakfast included, afternoon snacks available. No air-conditioning or fans.

Villa del Sol

———————

Mexico's most exotic Pacific Coast inn is the white plaster jewel, Villa del Sol, just steps from the incomparably white sand beach near Zihuatanejo. This bed-breakfast-and-dinner inn was built from the ground up by Helmut Leins, an engineer from Munich who fell in love with the area while vacationing. He found a stretch of protected beach for sale in 1978, pulled up his European roots, and plunged in.

The rooms are principally of hand-smoothed plaster and cedar from the mountains. "Drawers never work in the Mexican tropics," Helmut commented, explaining why his built-in plaster dressers hold loosely fitting rectangular baskets instead. Indeed, bed platforms, sofa bases, end tables, even towel racks are plaster. And he used no nails to secure the cedar.

His sixteen rooms are somewhat similar. Ours featured a tiled front patio with heavy Mexican woven hammock. Hand-crafted slatted doors slide across the front of each suite at night; during the day, they push back to expose a built-in sofa/seating area with a large coffee table. Up three steps and behind a low rail is the larger bedroom, dominated by a huge, fully canopied bed. Mosquito netting romantically cascades from tiebacks at each corner. A sea breeze and ceiling fans ward off insects.

The fully tiled bathroom has a walk-in shower with slanted floor and drain, and plenty of bars and hooks for towels and clothing.

A small side patio adjoins the bedroom. Its round hide-covered table and chairs are shaded by coconut palms that loom up from grounds laced by flower-edged paths. One path crosses a plaster-encased spear of blue water which leads to the swimming pool.

Meals are taken in the open under a palm-thatched *palapa*. Helmut has made the leather chairs more comfortable with cushions. The sunken bar, in the shape of a beached boat, dispenses the most exotic liquid refreshments, cheery barefooted waitresses sort out your broken Spanish, and the view is a vacation in itself. On one side, the pool sparkles; on the other, the white sand and gentle surf of scenic Zihuatanejo Bay are just a dozen steps away. There is even a lighted tennis court.

Helmut has imported a European chef for his restaurant, which also attracts diners from nearby Ixtapa hotels. The menu of the day, written on a chalkboard by the bar, utilizes local fresh foods as well as specialty items from Mexico City. Hours are a compromise between North American (early) and Mexican (late) traditions; supper is served 8:30 to 10 P.M. If you cannot eat the food offered on a particular night, the chef will prepare a special plate.

Breakfast is large, and its menu comprises many choices. Likewise, the blackboard for lunch lists several à la carte choices; but lunch is not included in your room price, and you probably will want to try other dining establishments during your daytime wanderings.

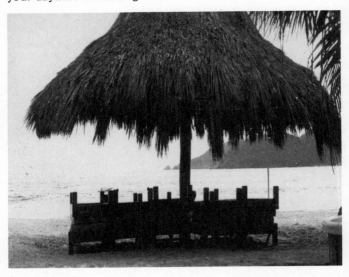

Villa del Sol, Apartado Postal 84, Zihuatanejo, Guerrero, Mexico. Telephone (operator assisted) 743-4-22-39. Helmut W. Leins, host. 16 rooms with baths. Expensive; price includes breakfast and supper. Overhead fans.

Padded lounge chairs dot the beach, and a water-ski boat is available for the hotel's guests. It's fun just to sit on the beach, which also serves as an informal business thoroughfare. You can buy the paper, fish, sandals, shells, and other goods from passing vendors. I spent a few hours swimming and sitting—feeling especially rewarded by the antics of a beautiful red setter surfing on the breakers—and knowing that all those uninformed tourists filling Ixtapa's highrise hotels can only look at their oceanfront. The Mexican government, in all its wisdom, built that resort on a piece of coastline with too much undertow for beaches, let alone swimming.

Returning from the beach to Villa del Sol, you know an engineer constructed this inn. Its entire length is railed, and you can enter its grounds only by walking through a shallow foot bath, designed to keep sand where it belongs. If Helmut could only invent something to catch the coconuts that quietly and unexpectedly fall all over, sometimes denting rented cars.

Another helpful touch is the humorous pamphlet describing the do's and don'ts at Villa del Sol. It's more like a letter to a friend, and it covers everything from restaurant hours to tipping to occasional nonfunctioning details, human and mechanical. It ends with an invitation to relax, Mexican style, and pick a hibiscus for your hair—but please, from the back of the bush so everyone can enjoy the ones in front.

And things here are relaxed. By the second day at Villa del Sol, you'll be down to wearing nothing more than a bathing suit. In fact, it was half a bathing suit for one young surfer.

Hotel El Mirador

A
nyone who has set foot in Acapulco has seen Hotel El Mirador, though few realize it. Remember riding past the north end of town to see the *quebrada* (ravine) divers? You were herded down some steps, sold soft drinks, and talked out of a few extra dollars for those brave divers. You stood on the corner of a tiered open-air restaurant and watched these daredevils dive from incredible heights into crashing waves. After twenty minutes, you were herded back to the bus or taxi.

You missed something. And I almost did, too.

We were planning to stay at a smaller Acapulco hotel suggested as a possible "find." It just didn't make it in the "romantic Mexican inn" category, though, so I went through my card file. El Mirador sounded clean, safe, and non-stainless steel, though awfully touristy.

The staffed parking lot—with everpresent sidewalk vendors and tour busses awaiting their passengers—was a turn-off, as were the boutiques along the arcade outside the hotel. But it was 6 P.M. and we were tired, so we trudged on. Fortunately, all that circus stuff ended at the lobby entry. A quick, youthful manager assigned us a room with an ocean view (they all have ocean views, we found later) and summoned a somewhat older bellboy to show the way. He is necessary even if you have light luggage, for El Mirador is a many-leveled wonder. Its countless low-slung, layered structures attach to the cliffside like so many mussels on a beach rock. These small two-and three-story white stucco and tile buildings hold 133 of the hotel's rooms. The nearby tower, new in 1985, holds another fifteen. Each is given a place name or a girl's name, and around each front door is painted a garland of brightly colored flowers. The same native Indian artist does all the painting.

Our room had been comfortably cooled beforehand, which is very important in a place as uncomfortably hot as Acapulco; otherwise you spend hours dripping perspiration. The entire half-century-old hotel has converted from ceiling fans and vented shutters to air-conditioning. But I forgot the heat once I saw the view. The deep room ended with a picture window and windowed door filled with nothing but ocean, sky, and horizon. That gets me every time. Forget the room, let's go sit on the patio and listen to the ocean pound the base of this rock outcropping.

White stucco walls keep the spacious patio private from those adjoining. You can sit at the table for two, sun yourself in the chaise lounge, or view the scene from the cute little scoop of a loveseat. You can watch the sunset during winter months, or light the chimney-protected candle for moonlight rendezvous.

If you sit at the patio's edge, you can see the point farthest out to sea, where young boys stand like shorebirds daring each other to dive and older men cast fishing nets. Closer, at the foot of the property, surf pours into the hotel's seawater pool and a small cupola over the waves serves as a bar. I later descended twisting staircases past a large freshwater pool and found this inlet taken over by little rock crabs and schools of tropical fish delicate marine blue in color. A tram/elevator lowers guests down the face of a cliff to this pool, just north of the ravine where divers perform.

Back in the room, heavy matching Indian carved furniture sits on earth-colored interlocking glazed tile. A single plank headboard unites the double and single beds, a good compromise between Mexican and North American sleeping preferences. In the remodeled clean white bathroom, by the entry door, light pours through opaque ceiling glass over beige fixtures and a glassed-in tub/shower. Some 1930s shower plumbing is still in place, but just for nostalgia. Beige towels here and beige sheets under brown and white random-splotch bedspreads show attention to color coordination.

I think there were people in the next room, but we heard nothing over the crashing waves. We didn't have to lock out the sound at night, either. We drew the drapes, adjusted the louvers in the locked patio door, and let soothing sounds from the Pacific lull us through the night.

But what about the restaurant? With all those busloads of tourists, the waiters must be surly, the food pedestrian. Not so. When we explained we were staying at the hotel, the smiles came out every time. We were seated away from the tourist viewing area, which is easy to do here—the cliffside La Perla restaurant has seven tiers. In the evening, we were seated in what would be the box seats of a theater and could see every dive. A perfectly cooked, tender chateaubriand steak for two was less than $20. Service was prompt but not hurried. Breakfast proved the same. It was a Saturday, and many businessmen gathered for their early meal. That says something for the food and service, which includes many refills of good coffee.

El Mirador was started in 1934 by a Hungarian, called Don Carlos Barnard by the Mexicans. Over the next twenty-five years, he'd add a wing here and a wing there to what was once a tent village. Renovations and improvements still go on, a little each year, just like before. Now, though, as a result of the country's monetary tailspin in 1981, the government owns the hotel—although you'd never know it. Employees, most of whom have worked there ten or more years, are proud of El Mirador and their part in it. Alberto Salas, the food and beverage manager, was born at the hotel.

The most spectacular room is Labertino, suite 114. On a

El Mirador, La Quebrada 74, Acapulco, Guerrero, Mexico. Telephone (operator assisted) 748-3-11-55 or -3-12-21; telex 16-833-557-88-22. Alejandro Aguirre, reservations manager. 148 rooms and suites, all with ocean view. Inexpensive May–December, moderate December–April. Air-conditioning.

point above "diver's rock," it has windows all around and a brick deck on each side as well. The double bed, under a flower-painted archway, faces this view. Soft blue carpets cover the floors in bedroom and sitting room, and the newly tiled bathroom is also blue.

This and the honeymoon suite, number 101, can each be had for around $75 per night. Other rooms with views of the divers are numbers 102 through 110.

So the next time you visit Acapulco, have the taxi driver take you to El Mirador—and leave you there.

Playa Hermosa

I f you wish to visit this hot, humid, crowded tourist trap of a city on Mexico's beautiful western coast, there is an inn hidden away from "hotel row" for you. A block from the public beach and between the downtown section and the hotels, Playa Hermosa's buildings sprawl along lawn areas and by a good-sized pool.

Simply furnished, all twenty-one rooms have private baths. The newer wing, rooms 18 through 21, is air-conditioned and nearer the pool. You really need air-conditioning in Acapulco to ensure comfort. Perhaps there are days that are exceptions, but better to be prepared.

Rooms are rather small, with two beds together under a wall hanging. White walls accent the furniture's dark wood. Bathrobes are provided, which is a blessing; otherwise, you'd devote a disproportionate amount of luggage space to a robe you need only a few times, such as when you walk to the pool. Playa Hermosa also sells T-shirts, just like the big highrise places farther around the bay.

Señor Lalo McKissak, owner, charges very little. Surprisingly, the low tariff includes a good-sized breakfast of fruit, eggs, and beverage; this is served either on an open patio to the rear of the large main structure, or in the lounge/library.

Playa Hermosa has an informal air. I'm sure one could meet the most interesting people while sunning on the lawn by the pool or choosing a book in the library. Activity-oriented visitors can charter fishing boats, sail, parasail, golf, or play tennis. The local museum of archeology may stimulate the more thoughtful.

Another advantage to Playa Hermosa is its proximity to practically everything in Acapulco. You can walk to the long stretch of public beach, only a block away, or to the swinging hotels and restaurants. For points farther off, buses and taxis continually parade up and down Costera Boulevard, which rings the beach.

This is about the only hotel in this book that is near an active night life. Most of Acapulco's larger hotels feature night-club acts from piano bars to flamenco shows to a spine-tingling native Indian performance in which men hang from ropes tied to a central pole and spin around over the heads of the audi-ence. Mexican vacationers love Acapulco as much as those from the States, so the night spots are usually jumping until midnight; Mexicans are accustomed to dining later, in the cool evening hours.

A visit to the public beaches taught me about the tenacity of Acapulco street vendors. I don't know where they get all

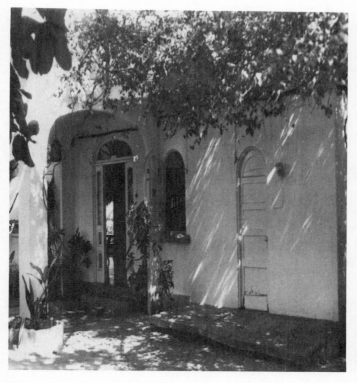

Playa Hermosa, Fracc Hornos, Acapulco, Guerrero, Mexico. Telephone (operator assisted) 5-14-91. Lalo McKissak, owner/ host. 21 rooms with baths. Inexpensive; breakfast included. Some rooms air-conditioned.

their peasant blouses, silver goblets, mother-of-pearl inlaid trinkets, lacy hats, thongs, necklaces, and other items, or how they carry them around all day. Fortunately, these independent business men, women, and children do not hang around Playa Hermosa. This is a blessing worth a great deal to me.

One point to remember: If you arrive at Playa Hermosa between 1 and 5 P.M., Señor Lalo is taking a siesta, as is most of Acapulco, and you are on your own with a Spanish-speaking staff.

9

Baja California

Baja California, the barren, isolated finger of land along the northwest coast of Mexico, has an image problem. Last to be visited by Spanish conquerors or Jesuit priests, it was more or less shunned by travelers. Cortés did sail to Baja California—and then sailed home again. Father Junipero Serra, who led the Christian settlement of California, passed right on through the land on his way to San Diego and points north.

No longer is Baja ignored by mobile adventurers. Now campers, trailers, recreational vehicles, and cars of all sizes travel the relatively new highway that goes all the way to Cabo San Lucas, its southernmost tip. (I'd rather visit the dentist than take that drive again. But mine is a minority opinion, judging by the number of U.S. license plates in Baja.) From California, Baja is the easiest part of Mexico to reach. This availability has done little to improve the ugly American image, though, or the impassive Mexican image.

Not that the country doesn't have charm. Encino is a lovely town, far enough from the border to be truly Mexican in flavor, and home of the only good winery in the country. Loreto, much smaller and unspoiled, is the oldest settlement on the peninsula. La Paz, the capital of Baja Sur, is a tidy city with a bustling port. Cabo San Lucas and nearby villages, though much changed by direct access roads from California, are still dramatic places to visit: the road ends there, two great bodies of water meet, and the fishing, snorkeling, and whale-watching are great.

Baja still has a problem with its self-image, however. Not many natives live there. In fact, many of the workers in tourist-trade jobs commute from the mainland. All view daily the disposable income of visiting tourists, while their own incomes leave something to be desired. Many appear sullen or resentful, an unnatural posture for these normally joyous people. Those with property are thinking up ways to lease it in small lots to North Americans wishing to build in Baja, especially between the border and Ensenada.

In Baja California, few inns have bottled water, forcing tourists to drink the strongly mineral flavored tapwater. It may be safe, but it does not have the same properties as tapwater at home and may cause problems. If you drive to Baja, stow a few bottles in the car for emergencies.

The north half of the Baja peninsula is in the Pacific Standard Time zone, while the south half is Mountain Standard, an hour earlier. This is confusing, since the whole rest of Mexico proper is on Central Standard time, from the Mexican Riviera to the Yucatán.

I found very few romantic inns on the peninsula, in proportion to the number of visitors it receives. Perhaps one reason is because of the relative newness of growth there. Still, I would return in a minute—as long as it didn't require a grueling two-or three-day drive each way.

But why risk the family car, or perhaps even the family, by droning down the Baja California highway, past 10 million cactus plants and jagged rocks, to reach the southern end of that beckoning index finger? Fly to La Paz, Cabo San Lucas, even Loreto, and wait for the diehard drivers while relaxing up to your chin in a refreshing swimming pool.

Hotel Palmilla

The pool at Hotel Palmilla, a resort located between Cabo San Lucas and the airport, is finished in tiny vibrant blue tiles, deeper in hue as the pool deepens, just like the ocean itself. The sea is just below, crashing onto a rocky promontory. If there were rocks on the grounds, you could throw one into the surf from poolside.

No chance of rocks at this manicured resort, though. Built in 1957 by Abelaego Rodriguez, owner of a private club near La Paz, the hotel's three structures hold forty-two rooms and hug 20,000 square meters of the rocky point. This is the southwestern edge of a white crescent of beach named Punta Palmilla (*palmilla* means "little palm trees"). Half a dozen chain-type hotels occupy the lower area, en route to the airport where flights arrive daily from Los Angeles, Tijuana, Mexico City, and often from Houston and Denver.

The approach to Hotel Palmilla is off the main highway and down a barely marked sandy road that narrows at a deceivingly small white arch; its wrought iron gate is closed nightly. When we inquired for directions at a restaurant outside the entry, the hostess wasn't quite sure this was the place. Of course, most guests either arrive by airport taxi or land their private planes at the hotel's own 6,000-foot gravel runway.

On a clue from friends, who had found the price is the same for all rooms, we asked for a king-sized bed. Rooms with oversized beds are all situated in corners and therefore slightly larger. They also have more view windows and lots of ventilation. Sure enough, our room—number 6 in the central arched building—must have been one of the nicest. On the lower level and facing the ocean, its expanse of slightly porous red tile flooring was satiny from wisps of fine salt spray tossed up by waves pounding the rocky buttress nearby. Wide sliding glass doors brought the outdoors in. Surprisingly, all that is necessary for temperature regulation is an overhead fan. Constant ocean breezes do the rest.

This room screamed luxury and, even rarer for south of the

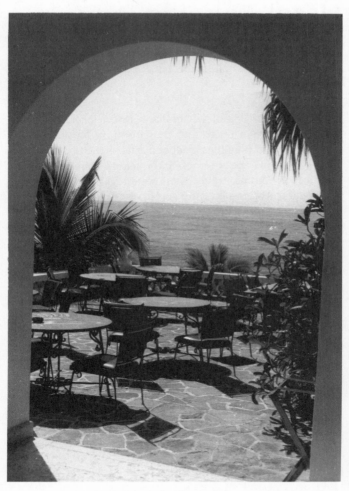

Hotel Palmilla, Apartado Postal 52, San José del Cabo, Baja California Sur, Mexico. Mario Cortez and Mario Gomez, resident managers. *For Reservations:* Atlas Travel House, 1904 Hotel Circle North, San Diego, CA 92108. Telephone (800) 854-2608 in the U.S.; (800) 542-6082 in California. 43 units by ocean. Expensive, but includes all meals. Overhead fans.

border, caring upkeep: no nicks, scrapes, or broken tiles. White stucco walls dramatize furnishings. The king-sized bed's carved headboard, like half a wagon wheel between smooth pillars, stands out in dark silhouette. A sitting area with heavy beige pillowed chairs adjoins the small fireplace and side window. Grouped with a round table, it makes a convenient spot for evening conversation. A rear el provides dressing room and closet space. The brightly tiled bath features a sunken shower whose spray head is a full seven feet from the floor, good news for tall men.

"We have no keys and no locked doors here," explained the manager. Store your valuables in the office safe.

The rather hefty tab at Hotel Palmilla includes all meals. Elegant and of excellent quality, they are more suggestive of a first-class U.S. restaurant than Mexican gourmet cuisine. Perhaps that is because practically everything is flown in from California: for supper, a small perfect steak wrapped in bacon, with blueberry cheesecake; for breakfast, strained orange juice, marvelous coffee in your own thermal pitcher, and eggs as you like; and for lunch, pounded and breaded chicken fillets, and kiwi pudding. The only dish of Mexican origin was an excellent vegetable soup with chicken broth.

The evening meal is served at linen-covered tables on a rail-lined patio overlooking the ocean. Pounding waves provide the background music, and the subdued lighting lets you see the moonlight glint on the water. What could be more romantic?

Breakfast and lunch are served in a tiled, windowed room the size of a basketball court. Square tables, each centered with a large mosaic of a colorful tropical fish, are set along the ocean side of the room, just out of reach of the hot sun. These tables may fill the room during the height of the season, but during our visit part of it stood empty and so appeared even larger.

Hotel Palmilla keeps most Baja trademarks at arm's length. Deep-sea fishing? Sure. But not at 4:30 in the morning on a bare skiff, as is the style in the rest of the country. Rather, the covered boat departs at 8 A.M. and carries a picnic lunch prepared by the kitchen staff.

You can enjoy other less demanding sports right on the grounds: under the coconut palms, twin croquet courts are surfaced with carpet; elsewhere are facilities for swimming, ping pong, shuffleboard, tennis, and snorkeling. And the magnificent bar, about two stories high and open to the ocean, has table games and is stocked with any sort of concoction you might wish.

Hotel Palmilla is actually like an adult summer camp. In fact, that's where its few faults lie, if one may be so presumptuous as to fault a place that charges about $175 a day for two people (including meals and taxes). Everything closes by 10 P.M. At 10:15 the exterior lights blink off. At 10:30 the gate is locked. Guests are in for the night, unless prior arrangements are made. In short, to make the most of this beautiful setting, be good ladies and gentlemen, and come prepared to supply your own entertainment.

Unlike summer camps and the other inns listed here, this resort's staff is cold and uncommunicative. The waitresses clattered dishes and chatted to each other in Spanish during our meals. Of course, when I explained the reason for my visit, a manager found time to answer questions. A California innkeeper who visited there had the same reaction.

All this may have improved. Since my visit, Hotel Palmilla has been sold. The new owners have already spent more than $3 million on upgrading and adding a VIP residence. Immediate plans are to add another unit with twenty rooms. Long-range objectives are to establish this as a world-class resort with 350 rooms, and areas for time-sharing and condominium ownership on the two miles of oceanfront.

It is difficult for me to imagine Hotel Palmilla $3 million better than it was the summer of 1984, and at the same price per person. All I can say is go now, before 300 more rooms are built!

Misiónes de La Paz

———————

Arriving in La Paz, we pointed an obliging rental car toward a reasonable sounding small hotel in the shadow of the great grey Hotel Gran Baja. But it was filled, and its manager asked, "Would you like to stay at an inn on an island?"

Does a fish like water? We were hooked. He made a call and then told us to take our bags down to the sandy beach in front of his hotel. Pretty soon a twenty-foot covered skiff threaded its way in past a few anchored pleasure boats, spotted us, and rammed its nose up onto the beach. Barefoot by then, we threw our light bags aboard; the pilot helped us in. And so it was that we went putting off into the sunset, the La Paz skyline visible over the stern and an island to be explored somewhere off the bow.

Well, not actually an island. Misiónes de La Paz is on the otherwise uninhabited peninsula that forms the outer arm of the La Paz harbor. In the fast darkening distance, there suddenly appeared a large white dome capped by a small cupola and bathed with light. As we drew nearer, we saw that, below the dome, the soft glow from innumerable bulbs illuminated a large octagonal room—a bar/restaurant/dance floor—windowed all around.

To the right, five smaller octagonal structures were divided into five quarters each. Most faced the lights of La Paz. If you stand in just the right place, many of these lights reflect in the large swimming pool.

What a magical introduction to a relatively new accommodation of note in Baja California!

The next surprise was in meeting the host, Gary Roberts, a six-foot-four Californian from Long Beach and Sacramento. Gary talked the Mexican owners of this striking place into opening it as an inn. Originally, the restaurant and rooms were the first segment of, and accommodated potential buyers in, a planned condominium development with boat slips. Further development has been shelved because of the *peso*'s devaluation.

We had time for a frothy *margarita* before dinner. The cocktail proved a lifesaver, the dinner was merely okay. Gary explained that both cooks called in sick that night, so he was the chef.

The dining room has a bright, informal feel, highlighted by red tablecloths on square tables and flamboyantly twisted white napkins waving like flags from wine glasses. Woven reed and stainless-steel spring chairs fill the area, which seven-panel bamboo screens separate from the entry and the bar. Dramatic Mexican soul music pours from a good sound system. And eight-foot-wide windows on five sides overlook twinkling shore lights across dark waters, with an obliging pelican perched on a pier in the foreground. Pretty romantic, all right.

The menu is extensive, with lots of seafood. As a nice touch, prices are on the gentleman's copy only. Gary stresses personal contact, much the way stateside innkeepers do (as patrons, we've heard from him twice since our stay), and the amiable waiter explains the specials in detail. We were captivated by our find, the sunset, the *tequila*, and life in general. A midnight swim later ended our storybook day.

The rooms, all new and air-conditioned, are arranged in a functional manner around a hollow core service area. Like segments in an orange slice, each fans out toward picture windows. The best views are in rooms ending with the digit three or four. King-sized beds, wet bars, tiled showers, and lots of tiled floor space make comfortable quarters for an extended stay for two, or for family groups, since the sofa is a fold-out bed. Sitting areas are set up both inside and on your own patio.

This is one of the few inns in Mexico whose bathrooms contain washcloths and individual cakes of soap. I don't know what this country has against washcloths.

By the second day, we'd become acquainted with Gary's three young sons, who help with the baggage, paperwork, and general feeling of informality. What is also great fun is the spontaneity: Gary held a weekend barbecue for hotel guests and others from La Paz. One, a vacationing Shriner who performs as a clown on occasion, donned his outfit at Gary's urging and became part of the entertainment.

You can decide to go shopping in La Paz on short notice, too. There's no charge for the seven-minute trip across the bay, except perhaps a tip for the skipper. Just tell him when to pick you up, then hop off the boat right there in the middle of town. And think of the convenience: no parking places to find, no taxis to summon. Since the boat is available twenty-four hours a day, the same goes for night life (centered in the hotels) or (free) tennis. A fleet of seagoing vessels is also on call here, so fishing is readily arranged, too. The fish are just outside the harbor entrance in the Gulf of California.

La Paz is an easy town to get around. Almost everything a visitor would want to see is within a few blocks of the waterfront, and streets are straight except for a small section that was probably the original town site. The large pink mission was built in the 1860s, and a museum explains Baja's history. If you don't get enough boating while at Misiónes de La Paz, a fun side trip is to ferry overnight to either Los Mochis or Mazatlán on the mainland.

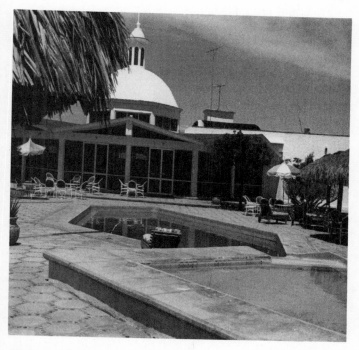

Misiones de La Paz, Apartado Postal 152, La Paz, Baja California Sur, Mexico. Telephone 1-706-822-0663; telex 52561-VIGAME. Gary Roberts, manager. 25 rooms. Inexpensive; kids under 12 free. Air-conditioned.

Hotel Misión de Loreto

———————

Dreams of John Steinbeck and *The Log from the Sea of Cortez* flicker through the minds of fishing enthusiasts who journey to the small town of Loreto in Baja California. With a small skiff, a sturdy pole and line, and a blue-finned marlin in mind, people go to tremendous lengths to reach this spot.

Surrounded by stark, sharp-ridged peaks, the historic town edges an incredibly blue bay, protected by Isla de Carmen, or Carmen Island. Off the breakwater rocks, snorkelers can see beautiful tropical fish. For $10 you can ride a skiff to the island's white sand beaches, which are as glittery as their Carribean counterparts. Shaded *cabañas* protect you from the constant sun.

Most people are out fishing, though.

Fishing boats for two or three people are available for around $60. Skiffs leave between four and five in the morning and fish until ll A.M. or noon, depending on the catch. Breakfast? Usually some eggs scrambled with bits of meat and wrapped in a tortilla, washed down by a lime soft drink. No wonder some *gringos* come back rather pale around the gills.

Many do return with fish, even in off season. By 2 P.M., after lunch, they join natives in *siesta*. Nonfishers either wilt or follow suit.

To rent fishing gear costs only a few dollars, but many people bring their own. Our Aeromexico flight from Los Angeles disembarked numerous long black fishing-pole canisters as we waited in the small thatched airport for our bags to be brought from the plane. Then we waited for the three available taxis to unload at various hotels and return for the next group of lucky visitors.

We first-timers were among the last picked up. Although the van was clearly labeled Hotel El Presidente, we were told to hop in. Hotel Presidente is one of the Mexican government's presents to tourists—a cavernous, luxurious oasis south of town, where the atmosphere is cold and commercial.

We wound up at Hotel Misión de Loreto, a friendly, comparatively efficient place about eighteen years old. It reopened in 1980 under new owners: a corporation. The three-story white U-shaped hotel is just behind the cement seawall that serves as the boardwalk of natives and tourists alike. In the evening as we joined the strollers, two bicycling boys hailed us with "¡Hola, good night!"

Only the first two floors are operational. The third was never finished. All overlook an oval pool with its little island and palm tree. This central courtyard also abounds with good-sized rubber trees, evergreens, and hibiscus. A whitewashed eyelet fence separates the patio and pool from the street, so you can see the blue water and purple hills of Carmen Island, beyond, but not be part of the show yourself. The exception is that little children can't resist peeking through the fence at the Americanos in the real swimming pool.

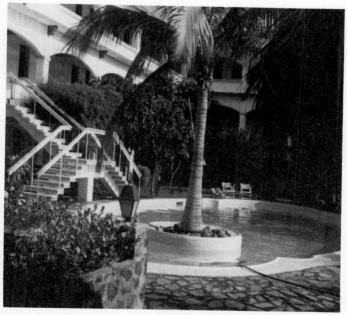

Hotel Misión de Loreto, P.O. Box 49, Lopez Mateo Bulevar, Loreto, Baja California Sur, Mexico. Telephone (operator assisted) 52-683-30048. 32 rooms and junior suites. Inexpensive. Some air-conditioned rooms.

You can walk about six blocks to the town square—slowly, for it's hot. There you'll find one of everything: market, pharmacy, police station, and mission. If you need to change money at the bank, which offers the best rate available, go between 9 and 11 A.M.

Late one afternoon we found a terrific seafood dinner on a dirt road near the unpaved square. Named Cesar's, it was in a small brick building with three air conditioners. We never would have found it, much less entered it, had not the hotel receptionist recommended it; as it was, we gorged on whole lobsters for under $5 apiece. The restaurant is no secret, though. In fact, it was filled with *gringos*.

This mission, for which the inn was named, is the oldest in Baja. Less grand than its mainland predecessors, it was founded in 1697 by Jesuit padre Juan María Salvatiera. Father Junipero Serra, founder of most of California's missions nearly 100 years later, started out from here. The museum signs are in Spanish, but the curator understands English. It's fun to watch grade-school boys race to see who will get to pull the ropes that ring the church bells.

Later, it's time to visit Los Pelicanos, the hotel's outside bar, for a good *margarita*. There, you sit on haystacks that have been sat on often before and watch a parrot swing himself side to side in his cage. Nice bartender, once you have attempted a few words in Spanish. Nice restaurant in the hotel, too. You can't miss if you order seafood.

Hotel Misión de Loreto is small enough to be by yourself, but you can talk to other guests if you wish. Rooms are comfortable and quiet. Two twin beds pushed together below a wide black rail headboard dominated our first-floor room. Each side had its own end table. There was no dresser, but the closet had shelves. A built-in loveseat partially filled the el by the door. Brown and beige bedspread and curtains over primitive French doors dictated the color scheme. The doors led to a small rear patio—all rooms have at least a small balcony—and matching windows opened onto the pool area.

The blue tiled bath featured a walk-in shower, clean blue fixtures, and a small, broken stained-glass window high in the wall. This comfortable junior suite, although very junior compared to some luxurious quarters described in this book, is most adequate for its low cost. It had air-conditioning, but not all rooms do; this is necessary in Baja during the hot summer months, and desirable all year, so specify when making a reservation.

10

Noted in Passing

This final catch-all chapter includes inns for which we do not yet have complete information. Some are famous and incredibly expensive, and some may be terrific bargains hiding behind plain exterior walls.

I have talked to many travelers who have packed the family car and driven to parts of Mexico with no plans in mind and certainly no reservations. Conversations usually zero in on glowing descriptions of a charming little *posada* in some little village where the owners took them in practically as one of the family. The name? They've forgotten. But it's six blocks past the Pemex, or a few kilometers down the road between x and y. Usually mentioned, too, is a similarly pinpointed counterbalance—a place to avoid at all costs. All this makes research a little difficult without good knowledge of the country and its language.

Even though the following half-dozen entries were briefly toured or recommended by others, it would take me another visit to gather enough material for a fair appraisal. Readers who visit any of these, or find another "charming little *posada*," please write to me in care of my publisher. And please include the inn's name, mailing address, and phone number for possible future inclusion.

Hotel Los Arcos *Taxco*

Abounding with arches, Hotel Los Arcos was built in 1620, the year the *Mayflower* arrived in North America. It was a nuns' convent for 200 years, then served in several silver-related functions—a factory, storage, and so on—before closing in 1972 for remodeling and today's tourists. Now comparatively complete, its twenty-four rooms go for about $14 a night for two people.

All meals are served under the arches downstairs by the open courtyard and foundation. The restaurant is leased to a woman who specializes in good old-fashioned Mexican food; she moderates the spicing for North American tastebuds.

A basement discotheque, now restyled for weekend entertainment for adults, features live music.

Hotel Los Arcos, Juan Ruiz de Alarcon No. 12, Taxco, Guerrero, Mexico. Telephone 52-732-2-18-36. Alfonso Ramirez Castillo, manager. 24 rooms. Inexpensive.

Posada Los Castillos   *Taxco*

Posada Los Castillos is a 15-room hotel on a steep, narrow street part way between Taxco's main square, where the buses unload, and the upper square, where the band shelter is. It was built in 1977 by a Señor Castillo who owns a large silver shop several doors away. You can walk around the railed landings of the hotel's four-story open stairway and look down at the tiled main floor,. or you can continue climbing to the rooftop skylight.

Splashes of orange accents, murals, and flowers against stark white walls and dark heavy Tascaro furniture make this a cheery place. Prints of round-faced Mexican children by José María Servin hang on walls of all rooms.

Our suite of two bedrooms and one bath cost $12 for two. This hotel has no restaurant, but Hotel Los Arcos, directly across the street, offers authentic Mexican food.

Posada Los Castillos, Juan Ruiz de Alarcon 7, Taxco, Guerrero, Mexico. Telephone (operator assisted) 52-732-2-34-71. Teodoro Contreras Galindo, manager. 15 rooms. Inexpensive.

Parador San Javier   *Guanajuato*

Parador San Javier is on an old *hacienda* two kilometers from Guanajuato (less than two miles). While a few of its rooms are in the historic *hacienda* and have fireplaces, most are in modern colonial-style units. Lovely gardens surround the buildings, and the dining room is said to be excellent. A heated pool, bar, and entertainment round out its amenities.

Parador San Javier, Plaza Aldama 92, Guanajuato, Gto., Mexico. Telephone (operator assisted) 2-06-26. 120 rooms. Moderate.

Hotel San Diego   *Guanajuato*

Across the street from Guanajuato's Hotel Castillo de Santa Cecilia is the more historic yet less spectacular Hotel San Diego. A heavy rectangular building with many small balconies, this venerable establishment houses fifty-five rooms in a modernized seventeenth-century convent. It also has a restaurant, bar, and entertainment. But it just doesn't have the *viva Mexico* of its neighbor. For once, the new outshines the old.

Hotel San Diego, Jardin de la Union 1, Apartado Postal 8, 36000 Guanajuato, Gto., Mexico. Telephone (operator assisted) 2-13-00. 55 rooms, many with semiprivate baths. Inexpensive.

Hotel Garza Blanca   *Puerto Vallarta*

About five miles south of Puerto Vallarta on both sides of the winding cliffside highway, Hotel Garza Blanca is a rather posh and expensive destination with a dining room, terrace, bar, pool, boat rentals, and one tennis court.

Guest accommodations are a combination of suites, cliffside chalets with pools, and a beachfront motel section (to be avoided). Nicest are the suites, in circular two-story bungalows with a parlor and bedroom. The best of these *casitas* are numbers 21 through 25.

This is one of the highest priced spots in this book, with a tab of $200 per couple per day in season.

Hotel Garza Blanca, Apartado Postal 58, 48300 Puerto Vallarta, Jalisco, Mexico. Telephone 322-2-10-23. 61 units in suites, bungalows, and motel. Expensive.

Las Hadas   *Manzanillo*

This huge white resort complex is at the end of a winding drive through golf courses and past private homes. It has its own inlet and is remote from downtown Manzanillo. More than 200 units are incorporated in various buildings, some two and three stories, others a half-dozen high. It has a posh look, down to electric carts that take guests to and fro between lobby and room, and perhaps to the beach. Tennis, golf, shops, three restaurants, and entertainment are on the grounds.

Las Hadas has a firm policy of privacy, allowing only those people with reservations inside the gate. Business cards, book contracts, and verbal scolding did not sway the official on duty the day we attempted entry. But I could tell from looking through the fence rails that anyone staying at Las Hadas wouldn't be in close contact with the ocean—or much semblance of real Mexico, for that matter.

Las Hadas, Apartado Postal 158, 28200 Manzanillo, Colima, Mexico. Telephone (operator assisted) 333-3-00-00. More than 200 units. Expensive.